THE TRADE AND
CLIMATE CHANGE NEXUS

THE TRADE AND CLIMATE CHANGE NEXUS

The Urgency and Opportunities for Developing Countries

Paul Brenton and Vicky Chemutai

 **WORLD BANK GROUP**

ISBN (paper): 978-1-4648-1770-0
ISBN (electronic): 978-1-4648-1773-1
DOI: 10.1596/978-1-4648-1770-0

Cover photos: © idreamipursue / iStock. Used with the permission of idreamipursue / iStock. Further permission required for reuse.
Cover design: Melina Rose Yingling, World Bank.

The Library of Congress Control Number has been requested.

Contents

Map

Tables

Foreword

All human and economic activities have an impact on the environment. Trade is no different.

The production, movement, and consumption of goods and services—within and across borders—is the foundation of modern society. This process brings us the energy that powers our homes and gets us to work each day. It delivers the food we need, the appliances we have come to depend on, and the medical supplies that help make us safer. Yet each stage of the process entails a fresh contribution to greenhouse gas emissions: trade undeniably exacerbates climate change. It is equally true that trade is disrupted by climate change. Extreme weather events often devastate transport and logistics infrastructure. These events erode capital stock, debilitate export capacity, damage agriculture, and disrupt food security—all with adverse consequences for long-term development outcomes.

Trade, in short, is a critical node to mobilize if the world is to achieve green, resilient, and inclusive development in the coming years. As this report demonstrates, it is a central element of the solution to climate change—because it has the potential to enhance mitigation as well as adaptation efforts. First, trade can help shift production to areas with cleaner production techniques: as the world makes the transition to a low-carbon economy, export comparative advantages will change, compelling countries to adapt and seize new opportunities. Second, trade promotes the spread of critical environmental goods and services that can help reduce emissions and improve environmental management—today, global trade in environmental goods is estimated at more than US$1 trillion annually and is rising. Third, imports are critical to immediate recovery from a natural disaster, when essential items such as food and medicines are in short supply. In a world increasingly shaped by climate change, trade will be a crucial mechanism to address food insecurity, support adaptation, and enable recovery from natural disasters.

In the last decade, some developing countries have emerged as fast-growing emitters of greenhouse gases. The poorest countries, however, remain the smallest contributors to emissions. Yet they often suffer the most from climate change. Natural disasters disproportionately affect the most vulnerable people and the smallest firms. All developing countries therefore have an important stake in adapting to climate change—especially in agriculture, which is central to food security, employment, and trade and is also the most sensitive to climate change. Tourism, the mainstay of the economy of many small island developing states, is also particularly sensitive to climate change. Diversifying away from sectors that are the most vulnerable to climate shocks will allow these economies to become more resilient over the long term.

The global community has an important role to play in greening trade. This report identifies several immediate trade policy measures that offer quick wins. Correcting the current bias in many countries' tariff schedules toward imports of carbon-intensive "dirty" goods is one of them. Advanced economies can also support green trade liberalization of goods and services of high-priority interest to exporters in developing countries. Multilateral negotiations should focus not only on tariffs on environmental goods but also on nontariff measures and regulations affecting services—access to which is often vital for implementing the new technologies embodied in environmental goods. Enforceable rules should be created to ensure global discipline in the use of trade measures that impede crisis response—such as export restrictions on food or medicine or restrictive intellectual property rights that prevent the diffusion of clean technologies to developing countries. The need for transparency and predictability in policies affecting trade is always pressing, but it is particularly urgent during a crisis.

The least-developed countries also need to be at the multilateral negotiating table for matters involving trade and the environment. Policy makers in these countries have not paid much attention to trade policy as a tool for achieving environmental objectives. By contributing to the rules governing environmental trade, they can ensure that their interests—especially regarding capacity building and data collection—are duly considered. They can help ensure that the standards set reflect the reality of production in these countries.

All developing countries have much to gain by improving their policies on trade and the environment. Implementing ambitious nationally determined contributions (NDCs) to achieve climate goals, for example, can help them exploit new trade opportunities arising from the implementation of NDCs in other countries. Reaping the gains from emerging trade opportunities will also require developing countries to address their high costs of trade: doing so can make them both competitive and resilient in the long term. Lowering tariff and nontariff barriers on imports that embody new technologies can drive productivity growth and adaptation. The global community can help developing countries adopt climate-smart agriculture and build capacity for trade-facilitation reforms. Mutual recognition agreements covering environmental goods and products can go a long way in helping exporters in developing countries meet the regulatory requirements of developed countries, thereby cutting time and costs.

As countries formulate policies for recovery from the COVID-19 (coronavirus) pandemic, the World Bank Group is supporting their efforts to embark on a green, resilient, and inclusive development path, setting the foundation for robust and sustainable growth and development in the longer run. The World Bank Group Climate Change Action Plan for 2021–2025 takes a *whole of economy* approach, focusing on policies to create the right enabling environment for climate action.

Trade is an indispensable requirement for achieving the global development agenda. This report provides a timely review of critical issues involving green trade, laying out the key policy steps that countries can take to ensure that trade plays its full role in supporting the transition to a low-carbon future.

Mari Pangestu
Managing Director of Development Policy and Partnerships
World Bank

Acknowledgments

The authors are indebted to many colleagues for their contributions to the substance of this report. These include Dabo Guan (distinguished professor, Tsinghua University, China, and University College London, UK), Michael Friis Jensen (consultant, Trade and Regional Integration Unit [ETIRI], World Bank), Maryla Maliszewska (senior economist, ETIRI), Maria Filipa Seara E Pereira (consultant, ETIRI), Israel Osorio-Rodarte (economist, ETIRI), Dominique Van Der Mensbrugghe (research professor and director, Global Trade Analysis Project Center at Purdue University), Walter Mandela (consultant, ETIRI), Mariam Soumare (consultant, ETIRI), Nyembezi Mvunga (consultant, ETIRI), Anita Nyajur (consultant, ETIRI), and Emilia Malavoloneque (consultant, ETIRI).

Many colleagues, inside and outside the World Bank Group, provided useful comments, suggestions, and inputs at various drafting stages: Michael Ferrantino (lead economist, ETIRI); Robert Mutyaba (climate change specialist, World Bank); Stéphane Hallegatte (lead economist, World Bank), and Kayenat Kabir (consultant, World Bank) on behalf of the Climate Change Group; and Emiliano Duch (lead private sector specialist, World Bank), Miles McKenna (associate economist, International Finance Corporation), and Brian Blankespoor (environmental specialist, World Bank). At the World Trade Organization (WTO), valuable comments were received from Aik Hoe Lim (director, Trade and Environment Division) and Daniel Ramos (legal officer, Trade and Environment Division).

The team also deeply thanks Erik Churchill (Vice President of Public Affairs, United Parcel Service, United States), Mohini Datt (consultant, ETIRI), Pratyush Dubey (consultant, ETIRI), Niels Junker Jacobsen (senior trade specialist, ETIRI), and Karen Souza Muramatsu (consultant, ETIRI) for their valuable recommendations. Administrative support was also provided by Tanya Cubbins, Victoria L. Fofanah, Aidara Janulaityte, and Flavia Nahmias da Silva Gomes.

We are also grateful for the insights and collaboration of several colleagues who have participated in the Trade and Climate Change Webinar Series. These include Richard Damania (chief economist, Sustainable Development, World Bank), Vicente Hurtado Roa (head of unit, Directorate-General for Taxation and Customs Union, European Commission), Georg Zachmann (senior fellow, Bruegel), Holger A. Kray (practice manager, Agriculture and Food Security, World Bank), Edwini Kessie (director, Agriculture Division, WTO), Steven Stone (chief, Resources and Markets Branch Economy Division, United Nations Environment Programme), Grzegorz Peszko (lead economist, Environment and Natural Resources, World Bank), Lourdes Sanchez (senior policy adviser and lead on Indonesia, International Institute for Sustainable Development), Shari Friedman (agriculture global head, Climate Strategy and Business Development, International Finance Corporation), Penny Naas (president, International Public Affairs and Sustainability, United Parcel Service, United States), Steve Nicholls (head of environment, National Business Initiative, South Africa), Urvashi Narain (lead environmental economist for East and Southern Africa Region, World Bank), Ryan Abman (assistant professor of economics, San Diego State University), Clark Lundberg (research agricultural economist, Economic Research Service, US Department of Agriculture), Michele Ruta (lead economist, ETIRI), Prudence Sebahizi (chief technical adviser on the African Continental Free Trade Area, African Union Commission), Allen Asiimwe (chief technical officer, Trademark East Africa), Olivier Mahul (practice manager, Crisis and Disaster Risk Finance, World Bank), Alexei Kireyev (senior economist, International Monetary Fund), Andrew Burns (lead economist, EMFMD, World Bank), Aik Hoe Lim (director, Trade and Environment Division), Ronald Steenblik (senior fellow, International Institute for Sustainable Development), Mahesh Sugathan (senior policy adviser, Forum on Trade, Environment, and the Sustainable Development Goals; independent consultant), Kimberley Botwright (community lead, Global Trade and Investment, World Economic Forum), Ana Laura Lizano (trade counselor, Permanent Mission of Costa Rica to the World Trade Organization), Martha Martinez Licetti (practice manager, ETIMT, World Bank), Stefan Gössling (professor, Department of Service Management and Service Studies, Lund University; School of Business and Economics, Linnaeus University, Kalmar), Kimarli Fernando (chairperson, Sri Lanka Tourism), and Megan Morikawa (global director for sustainability, Iberostar Group).

The authors are deeply grateful to Anna Brown, Elizabeth Forsyth, and Inge Pakulski, who edited the text. Patricia Katayama and Mark McClure expertly led the publishing process. Yaneisy Martinez coordinated the print and electronic conversion. Melina Rose Yingling created the cover and interior design.

Elizabeth Price and Inae Rivers provided excellent guidance on the communications strategy, and Avik Ray created the video for this report.

All information on the trade and climate change work program is posted on the World Bank website at https://www.worldbank.org/en/topic/trade/brief/trade-and-climate-change.

This report is an output of the Trade and Regional Integration Unit of the World Bank. Funding support was received from the Umbrella Trust Fund for Trade, which is supported by the Foreign, Commonwealth & Development Office (FCDO), the State Secretariat for Economic Affairs of Switzerland (SECO), the Ministry of Foreign Affairs of Norway, the Ministry of Foreign Affairs of the Netherlands, and the Swedish International Development Cooperation Agency (Sida).

The former global director for Trade, Investment, and Competitiveness, Caroline Freund (now Dean, School of Global Policy and Strategy, University of California at San Diego) and Antonio Nucifora, ETIRI practice manager, provided valuable guidance and supervision throughout.

About the Authors

Paul Brenton is lead economist in the Trade and Regional Integration Unit of the World Bank. He focuses on analytical and operations work on trade and regional integration. He has led the implementation of World Bank lending operations such as the Great Lakes Trade Facilitation Project in the Democratic Republic of Congo, Rwanda, and Uganda. He coauthored the joint World Bank–World Trade Organization report *The Role of Trade in Ending Poverty*, and has managed a range of policy-oriented volumes, including *De-Fragmenting Africa: Deepening Regional Trade Integration in Goods and Services*; *Africa Can Help Feed Africa*; and *Carbon Footprints and Food Systems: Do Current Accounting Methodologies Disadvantage Developing Countries?* He joined the World Bank in 2002; before that, he served as senior research fellow and head of the Trade Policy Unit at the Centre for European Policy Studies in Brussels and lectured in economics at the University of Birmingham (UK). A collection of his work has been published in *International Trade, Distribution, and Development: Empirical Studies of Trade Policies* (https://www.worldscientific.com/worldsci-books/10.1142/9172). Many of his research and policy papers are available at http://ideas.repec.org/f/pbr273.html. He has a PhD in economics from the University of East Anglia.

Vicky Chemutai is a Young Professional with the Trade and Regional Integration Unit of the World Bank. Her interests include analyzing the dynamics of international trade and its interactions with global issues—among others, climate and gender concerns. She has developmental experience spanning the public sector in several Ugandan government agencies (health, social security, and the central bank); the private sector as founder of several small-scale entrepreneurial ventures; and the international development sector, focusing on trade policy formulation and implementation, formerly at the World Trade Organization and currently at the World Bank Group. She has been an adjunct lecturer at the International University in Geneva in the fields of trade and statistics and has coauthored publications on trade policy and its impacts on countries' development. She holds an MSc in international trade policy and trade law from Lund University (Sweden), an advanced postgraduate diploma in international trade policy and trade law from the Trade Policy Training Centre in Africa (Tanzania), and a BSc in quantitative economics from Makerere University (Uganda).

Executive Summary

While trade contributes to climate change, *it is also a central part of the solution—enhancing both mitigation and adaptation.* This report explores the ways in which trade and climate change intersect. In the process, it confronts several myths concerning trade and climate change (as summarized in table ES.1). Trade exacerbates the emissions that cause global warming and is itself affected by climate change through changing comparative advantages. The report focuses on the impacts of, and adjustments to, climate change in low- and middle-income countries and how both the changing climate and the policy responses to address it will affect future trade opportunities.

Low- and middle-income countries are at the heart of the nexus between trade and climate change, facing severe challenges but also opportunities in the transition to a low-carbon future. Trade-driven growth will be essential to eliminating extreme poverty; however, given existing structures of production, this growth will also drive increasing emissions. Both adaptation and the shift to a lower-carbon growth trajectory will be key challenges for the most vulnerable countries, which have the least resources and weakest capacity to adjust to a changing climate. An increasing body of analysis shows that low-carbon and climate-resilient growth can provide poverty reduction and human development outcomes superior to the current alternative. In this context, the World Bank Group is supporting countries to embark on a *green, resilient, and inclusive development* (GRID) path, in which trade must play a key role, especially as a conduit for making new low-carbon technologies available to low- and middle-income countries.

Trade is increasingly being affected by extreme weather-related shocks such as storms, floods, and droughts, but it is often critical to the recovery from such events. Exports and imports are directly affected negatively when trade-related transportation and logistics infrastructure sustains significant damage. Longer-term adverse impacts arise from loss of life and injury of employees and damage to buildings, machinery, and so forth. These impacts are compounded when exporter contracts are canceled because companies cannot fulfill orders during the crisis. Food production is hit hard when extreme weather events prevent the planting or harvesting of main crops. Imports are critical to the immediate recovery from a natural disaster. Trade allows imports from unaffected countries to meet the crisis-induced shortage of supply in critical goods and services. Such imports are crucial to avoiding long-term negative development outcomes. For example, imports of food can prevent malnutrition and

TABLE ES.1   The Trade and Climate Change Myth Buster

The myth	The emerging reality
Trade is bad for the environment.	Trade flows contribute to carbon emissions but are also a critical part of the solution to climate change for three major reasons: (1) trade shifts production to areas with cleaner production techniques; (2) trade promotes the spread of environmental goods and services necessary for transitioning to low-carbon production; and (3) trade delivers critical goods and services that are vital in periods of recovery from extreme weather events.
Trade is bad for climate change relative to domestically produced goods because of the emissions from international transportation.	While the international transportation of goods and services is a source of emissions, other sources of carbon competitiveness along the value chain can more than offset its quantity of emissions. For example, fruits and vegetables produced in Africa using sunshine, manual labor, and natural compost may generate far fewer emissions than production in Europe requiring heated greenhouses, tractors, and manufactured fertilizer.
Because they are not large emitters individually, the poorest countries do not need to play a major role in negotiating the rules on trade and environment.	Collectively, low- and middle-income countries have been increasingly carbonizing over the last decade in pursuit of their development goals, and they need to be at the forefront of climate change adaptation and mitigation. Climate change will affect the poorest countries most severely, and contributing to the rules governing trade and the environment can help to ensure that their interests are considered properly.
If a country gets its climate policy right, then the job is finished.	Trade and climate change policies intersect. Trade reforms in the absence of appropriate climate change policies can have adverse impacts on emissions. When appropriate climate change policies are implemented, trade reforms ensure that goods and services are produced in the most (carbon) efficient location.
There is no need to review tariffs from a climate change perspective.	Tariff structures are often biased in favor of dirty goods. Bringing tariffs on dirty goods in line with those on clean goods would make a significant contribution to reducing carbon emissions.
The impacts of climate change will not be felt soon, so mitigation policies suffice for now.	Rising temperatures and changing patterns of precipitation are already affecting crop yields and traditional comparative advantages. Mitigation is necessary, but not sufficient; adaptation will be critical, especially for poor countries.
While nontariff barriers increase trade costs, they have little to do with climate change.	Nontariff barriers are a major constraint on trade in critical environmental goods. They also limit access to key products that will drive adaptation, such as seeds and fertilizers. Delays at the border and in ports indirectly exacerbate the huge waste of food products, with the resulting cost of higher emissions for a given level of food consumption.

Source: World Bank.

stunting of children, which affects their learning and productivity in later life. During reconstruction, imports provide the equipment, materials, and skills needed to rebuild the capital stock and transportation infrastructure.

Climate change is also affecting traditional comparative advantages, specifically agriculture and tourism, which are of particular importance to many low- and middle-income countries—more than industrial activities. The vulnerability of agricultural yields to climate threatens not just domestic food security but also the economic development of food-exporting countries and their ability to eliminate poverty. Yet outcomes are not always negative and vary across and within countries. Most studies of climate change and its impacts on agriculture have focused on crop production, but the effect of heat on labor productivity will also reduce agricultural output. In the tropics, the impacts of heat stress may be greater on humans than on adapted crops. With regard to tourism, climate change is increasingly undermining its role in driving development and reducing poverty in vulnerable countries, such as small island developing states.

Substantial new opportunities are emerging for low- and middle-income countries to diversify exports in a low-carbon global economy. While these countries face huge challenges in adapting to climate change, they will be able to benefit from natural low-carbon advantages and the application of new, low-carbon technologies to increase their carbon competitiveness as traditional comparative advantages are undermined.

In an increasingly climate change–afflicted world, trade will gain importance as a mechanism to address food insecurity, support adaptation, and enable recovery from extreme weather events. A trend toward deglobalization would compromise countries' ability to drive down poverty and transition to low-carbon growth. In fact, opportunities exist to reduce barriers to support the greening of trade and facilitate countries' adjustment to changing comparative advantages. Such measures include the following:

- Review country tariffs and remove any bias toward dirty sectors
- Reduce restrictions on access to environmental goods and services and on environmentally preferable products; accelerate negotiations on these goods and services at the multilateral level
- Remove nontariff barriers and implement trade facilitation and logistics reforms to reduce delays at borders and along trade routes, especially to reduce food waste and so contribute to food security
- Work collectively to develop standards on the carbon emissions embodied in a product that capture the realities of measurement in low- and middle-income countries; scale up technical assistance and capacity building on carbon measurement techniques and traceability
- Reduce tariffs and nontariff barriers on agricultural inputs and facilitate access to new technologies for farmers through expedited procedures for releasing seeds and easier movement of agricultural specialists
- Use the tools available at the World Trade Organization to address the climate change emergency, such as a waiver for the trade-related aspects of intellectual property rights of green technologies.

The use of export restrictions is particularly detrimental in a world marked by recurring climate disasters. Measures that reduce trade flows in countries less affected by a weather-related crisis undermine the efforts of countries battling an extreme weather event. These negative effects are increased in a world where specialization through trade and concentration of production in a few locations limit the options to substitute suppliers. Global food security is being increasingly compromised by the rising volatility of food supply at the country level as weather becomes more variable and uncertain.

This report offers two main suggestions for addressing these challenges. First, enhance efforts to increase information, transparency, and monitoring on global markets for essential items, including food. Greater transparency and information sharing can help to limit panic-driven policy decisions and lead to more informed and coordinated responses that avoid damaging trade restrictions. Second, deepen cooperation at the regional and multilateral levels on trade issues that are critical for health and food security and provide effective disciplines regarding the use of export-restricting measures.

It is critical to ensure that the interests of low- and middle-income countries are reflected in the design of trade measures introduced to reduce a country's or a company's carbon footprint. Governments are planning to introduce taxes at the border to complement domestic carbon taxes and prevent carbon leakage. Companies are also designing and implementing programs to demonstrate that they have reduced emissions along their value chains. There is no easy and commonly accepted way to calculate the carbon footprint of a product arriving at the border. Despite the difficulties, this calculation is required to tax the embedded carbon, as is information on carbon taxes (if any) already levied in the country of production. These programs face a range of practical implementation problems beyond measuring carbon content, including sector coverage, scope of carbon measurement, when and which default values are used, and how countries can demonstrate their carbon competitiveness. These measures all determine the impact of the program on the trade of low- and middle-income countries.

Measures to reduce carbon emissions will most heavily affect the countries that export fossil fuels and carbon-intensive products, but new opportunities will also arise in global value chains that are less carbon intensive. Measures to support climate mitigation objectives, including carbon border adjustment mechanisms, will increase the importance of export and output diversification in countries reliant on exports of fossil fuels and carbon-intensive manufactures, such as metals and fertilizers. But opportunities will arise for countries that can demonstrate carbon competitiveness in these manufacturing sectors. New opportunities will also arise as demand shifts to products that are less carbon intensive, such as electronics and other light manufacturing. But many low- and middle-income countries lack appropriate capacities to identify areas of carbon competitiveness, and their firms are unable to measure and verify carbon reductions for a given good or service. As a result, exports from low- and middle-income countries risk being taxed unfairly at the border, and their firms risk being excluded from international value chains.

It is essential for low- and middle-income countries to understand the risks and opportunities for trade and development strategies associated with climate change. This report offers a trade and climate policy diagnostic template that can provide inputs to country climate and development reports and beyond, to facilitate a broad dialogue on (1) strengthening capacities to identify opportunities for carbon mitigation that increase competitiveness, (2) investments in carbon measurement that are necessary to verify carbon competitiveness, and (3) trade policy and trade facilitation reforms that will support adaptation and access to essential technologies and techniques. This template brings together information on the trade and climate interlinkages at the country level to identify (a) key vulnerabilities in trade to rising temperatures, changing precipitation, and more frequent extreme weather events; (b) areas where trade can support mitigation and adaptation to a changing climate as well as emerging constraints; (c) regulatory gaps in the climate and trade policy environment; and (d) recommendations of climate-relevant trade policy options.

Abbreviations

ACCTS	Agreement on Climate Change, Trade, and Sustainability
AfCFTA	African Continental Free Trade Area
AGOA	African Growth and Opportunity Act
AMIS	Agricultural Market Information System
APEC	Asia-Pacific Economic Cooperation
ARIO	adaptive regional input-output
CAFTA	Central America Free Trade Agreement
CBAM	Carbon Border Adjustment Mechanism
CGE	computable general equilibrium
CO_2	carbon dioxide
CORSIA	Carbon Offsetting and Reduction Scheme for International Aviation
CPC	Central Product Classification
EBA	Everything But Arms
EC	European Commission
EEA	European Economic Area
EGA	Environmental Goods Agreement
EKC	Environmental Kuznets Curve
EPP	environmentally preferable product
ETS	Emissions Trading System
EU	European Union
GAINS	Greenhouse Gas–Air Pollution Interactions and Synergies (model)
GATS	General Agreement on Trade in Services
GATT	General Agreement on Tariffs and Trade
GDP	gross domestic product
GRID	green, resilient, and inclusive development
GSP	Generalized System of Preferences
GTAP	Global Trade Analysis Project
GVA	gross value added
ICAO	International Civil Aviation Organization
IFPRI	International Food Policy Research Institute
IMO	International Maritime Organization
IO	input-output
IPCC	Intergovernmental Panel on Climate Change

ISO	International Organization for Standardization
LULUCF	land use, land-use change, and forestry
MRIO	multiregional input-output
NDC	nationally determined contribution
ND-GAIN	University of Notre Dame Global Adaptation Initiative
OECD	Organisation for Economic Co-operation and Development
PAS	Publicly Available Specification
PPP	purchasing power parity
R&D	research and development
SBTi	Science Based Target Initiative
UNCTAD	United Nations Conference on Trade and Development
UNEP	United Nations Environment Programme
W/120	Sectoral Classification List
WTO	World Trade Organization

All dollar amounts are US dollars unless otherwise indicated.

1

Introduction

Climate change is increasingly at the forefront of domestic and international policy priorities, and solutions are urgently needed. Trade plays an important role in the emission of greenhouse gases that exacerbate climate change through its effects on the location and scale of production, consumption decisions, emissions from the international transporting of goods and services, and the transfer of technologies that may lead to lower emissions in production. Most recent estimates show that around a quarter of all global emissions are linked to international trade flows. While attention is currently focused on reducing emissions, it is increasingly recognized that the climate is already changing and that solutions to adapt to rising temperatures and more extreme weather events are urgently needed. According to the World Meteorological Organization (WMO), the summer of 2021 has seen intense and unprecedented heat waves, especially in the Northern Hemisphere.[1] Additionally, the WMO reports that from 1970 to 2019, weather, climate and water hazards accounted for 50 percent of all disasters, 45 percent of all reported deaths and 74 percent of all reported economic losses, with 91 percent of the deaths occurring in developing countries (WMO 2021b). Moreover, several climate economists have made projections and stressed the urgency of acting now, insisting that policy makers act in the coming decades, as these years represent a window of opportunity to develop smart and forward-looking adaptation policies.[2]

The poorest countries have not traditionally featured in the top list of carbon dioxide (CO_2) emitters, but they will face, or are already facing, the most adverse consequences, and these consequences will impede their growth and development. China, the European Union, India, Japan, the Russian Federation, and the United States accounted for about 70 percent of global emissions in 2019, but low- and middle-income nations are especially vulnerable and on the receiving end of climatic distortions. From cross-country analysis, Dasgupta et al. (2011) find a significant increase in the exposure of these countries to climate-induced changes in sea-level rise and storm surges. Malawi annually lost up to 1.7 percent of its gross domestic product (GDP) between 2005 and 2010 owing to extreme climate events (Pauw, Thurlow, and van Seventer 2010), and up to 12 percent of the population in Lilongwe District could be vulnerable to food insecurity by the end of the century (Stevens and Madani 2016). In Pakistan, a 1°C increase in temperature is estimated to lead to a substantial reduction in net farm revenue each year (Shakoor et al. 2011).

The effects of climate change are not always negative, but governments need to ready themselves for the incoming adjustments and figure out how best to adapt. The main changes in climate will take the form of rising temperatures, changing patterns of precipitation, more frequent river floods, sea-level rise, melting ice caps, and other extreme weather conditions—all having a direct impact on *how* and *what* the world trades: how trade will be affected—that is, over land, by plane, or by ship—and what trade will be affected, particularly in response to changing comparative advantages and patterns of production. The consensus among climate change analysts is that rising temperatures will likely have a positive impact in colder areas, by boosting agricultural productivity,[3] but will have a negative impact in hotter areas, especially in the tropics. A few studies have estimated positive changes, particularly in terms of transportation routes and transportation infrastructure (Heininen, Exner-Pirot, and Plouffe 2015). Arctic sea ice is already melting and opening new shipping routes, allowing ships with light icebreakers to navigate the Arctic Ocean more easily (Shiryaevskaya, Lombrana, and Tanas 2020). Within countries, the impacts of rising temperature and changes in rainfall patterns may be quite localized. For example, in Tanzania, while agricultural yields may rise in certain districts, they are expected to fall in others. Thus, impacts could differ across households both by region and by income category (Arndt et al. 2012). Understanding these changes would enable governments to design appropriate climate change adaptation policies.

As the private sector will be at the forefront of adaptation within the policy framework to be defined by governments, it needs to be engaged in policy discussions from the outset. Most private sector actors in the poorest countries tend to view climate change as an "environmental issue" rather than as a business issue with significant implications for them. Consequently, much of the private sector underrates the degree of climate risks (Goldstein et al. 2018). Any messaging needs to take this misperception into account, stressing the dire economic consequences of climate change, particularly for production and supply chains. In this regard, early engagement is critical. Governance mechanisms would be better off taking the form of public-private dialogues with civil society such that climate change adaptation becomes an integral part of decision-making at all levels of society (Fayolle et al. 2019). Therefore, it will be important to assess the degree of climate risks along the production and supply chains of private sector investments that are highly vulnerable to climate change.

Country-specific interventions regarding trade liberalization would be better informed if they were based on an in-depth analysis of the nexus between international trade and climate change. For example, any trade-related interventions targeted at boosting agricultural productivity and consequently increasing farmers' incomes would be remiss to ignore the criticality of drought-resilience strategies (Alfani et al. 2019). Additionally, Nhemachena and Hassan (2007), in assessing farmers' adaptation strategies for climate change in Southern Africa, find that farmers' access to credit and extension services as well as climate change awareness are important determinants of farm-level adaptation. Moreover, Ouraich et al. (2019), in analyzing Morocco and Turkey, conclude that the greater the trade liberalization, the higher the gains in global welfare, although these gains may not be large enough to offset the negative impacts on agricultural productivity globally. Clearly, any mitigation or adaptation strategy needs to take into account country-specific development needs as well as the prevailing institutional and technical capacity to address climate change. But policy makers also need to be aware of how climate change will affect other countries in terms of competitiveness and comparative advantage.

Good governance and appropriately designed policies today will be critical to realizing the benefits of trade while mitigating climate change, especially for low- and middle-income countries tomorrow. Emerson et al. (2011), in examining the nuances between trade and the environment, find that higher trade flows are correlated positively with good environmental practices and that good, data-driven decision-making will be fundamental to overcoming the existing challenges. The World Bank's flagship report on managing the impacts of climate change on poverty suggests that appropriate, climate-informed policies today will determine future impacts on poverty (Hallegatte et al. 2016). Governments of low- and middle-income countries often prioritize economic growth and poverty reduction. In view of this, when interacting with the Bank's client governments, addressing climate change should be considered a necessary conduit for catalyzing sustainable trade growth.

Trade in low- and middle-income countries will be affected by policy measures and private sector actions that are introduced to mitigate carbon emissions in other countries. Many countries are implementing policies to achieve their nationally defined contributions under the Paris Agreement, while being encouraged to set higher goals given the increasing evidence of the extent to which the planet is warming. Many of these policies, such as putting a price on the use of carbon through emissions-trading programs, will affect the structure of demand away from carbon-intensive goods and indirectly affect trade. More direct impacts will come if countries impose border adjustment programs to ensure that imports are taxed equally on their carbon content. Firms, too, are assessing their carbon footprint and seeking ways to reduce the emissions associated with them and to communicate their efforts to the wider society. Firms in low- and middle-income countries that supply inputs to global value chains may find that their buyers are placing more emphasis on the ability to track and reduce carbon emissions from their specific activities.

Hence, trade is a key element in discussions about climate change, touching on emissions, mitigation, and adaptation. Figure 1.1 presents an overview of the types of trade and environmental or climate policies addressed in this report. It shows the importance of creating policies that consider both trade and climate change issues. The dialogue underpinning these policies requires a strong analytical base that, while recognizing emissions related to trade and legitimate concerns over carbon leakage,[4] does not resort to populist views that treat trade in generic terms as "simply bad for climate change." In particular, these discussions need to recognize the gains from trade, how these gains can improve the ability of countries to invest in mitigation, and the instrumental role of trade in combating and adapting to climate change. While there are notable cases where trade has exacerbated environmental outcomes in countries with weak governance structures, there are also cases, such as Costa Rica, where trade liberalization has accompanied an improving environment.

This report shows that low- and middle-income countries are at the heart of the nexus between trade and climate change. Trade has been a phenomenal driver of poverty reduction over the past 30 years, and poverty reduction will remain the dominant development objective for many countries in the coming decades. But the changing climate and the policy responses being adopted to address it mean that current growth paths are not sustainable. Opportunities exist to move to a green, resilient, and inclusive development path, and trade will play a key role for many countries in this

FIGURE 1.1 Links between Climate Change and Trade

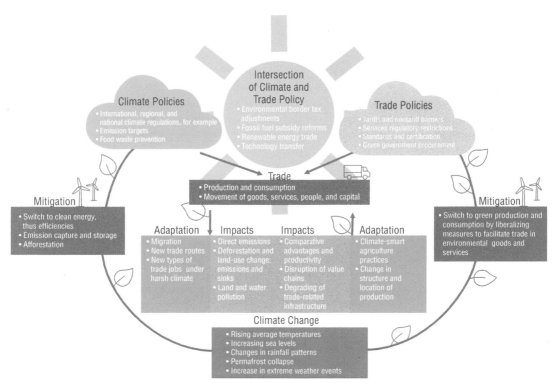

Source: World Bank.

transition. Indeed, there are good reasons to believe that greening trade will contribute more to better growth, poverty reduction, and human development outcomes than current development trajectories.

The report is organized as follows. Chapter 2 explains the rationale for paying attention to the important role of low- and middle-income countries in mitigating and adapting to climate change. It presents new analyses pointing to the increasing annual growth rate of emissions in the poorest countries and provides solutions that center on trade policy. Noting the importance of agriculture for low- and middle-income countries, this chapter also examines emissions related to land-use change and options for sustainable agricultural land management through trade policy. Chapter 3 delves into the evolving comparative advantages and discusses the impacts of extreme weather events. It uses a stylized model to illustrate the importance of refraining from the use of trade restrictions during climate disasters that are coupled with other global disasters, such as the COVID-19 pandemic. Chapter 4 presents the necessity of adaptation policies and the role of trade policy in facilitating the exchange of green goods and services and in promoting access to low-carbon technologies. It also discusses the implications of adaptation for trade. Chapter 5 examines the various types of environmental policies (at the government and firm levels) and their intersection with trade, especially regarding their effects on exports from the poorest countries. It also discusses the necessity of greening transportation, particularly for exports from poor countries, which are mostly agricultural. Finally, chapter 6 highlights some of the issues raised in applying the climate and trade policy diagnostic framework for Ethiopia and Vietnam. This report offers critical insights into the emerging types of climate-related issues and the corresponding trade policy options needed to present solutions. In doing so, it supports the World Bank Climate Action Plan (2021–25) and regional climate action plans. It is hoped that these findings will contribute to the dialogue between the World Bank and its client countries on trade and climate change issues.

Notes

1. For more details, see WMO (2021a), which adds that 2020 was one of the three warmest years on record. Further, June 2021 was the fifth-warmest June—and the warmest for Earth's land areas—since global record-keeping began in 1880, with temperatures 0.88°C (1.58°F) above the 20th-century average, according to National Oceanic and Atmospheric Administration's National Centers for Environmental Information.

2. For example, see Arndt et al. (2014) for their evaluation of the implications of climate change for growth and development in Malawi.

3. However, the positive impact on agricultural productivity could be offset by excessive rainfall or the emergence of pests.

4. *Carbon leakage* occurs when a mitigation policy in one jurisdiction leads not only to lower emissions in that jurisdiction but also to higher emissions in other, less climate-friendly jurisdictions, as firms shift their production to areas with less-stringent climate regulations.

References

Alfani, Federica, Aslihan Arslan, Nancy McCarthy, Romina Cavatassi, and Nicholas Sitko. 2019. "Climate-Change Vulnerability in Rural Zambia: The Impact of an El Niño-Induced Shock on Income and Productivity." FAO Agricultural Development Economics Working Paper 19-02, Food and Agriculture Organization, Rome.

Arndt, Channing, William Farmer, Kenneth Strzepek, and James Thurlow. 2012. "Climate Change, Agriculture, and Food Security in Tanzania." Policy Research Working Paper 6188, World Bank, Washington, DC.

Arndt, Channing, Adam Schlosser, Kenneth Strzepek, and James Thurlow. 2014. "Climate Change and Economic Growth Prospects for Malawi: An Uncertainty Approach." *Journal of African Economies* 23 (Suppl. 2): ii83–ii107. http://jae.oxfordjournals.org/content/23/suppl_2/ii83.full.

Dasgupta, Susmita, Benoit Laplante, Siobhan Murray, and David Wheeler. 2011. "Exposure of Developing Countries to Sea-Level Rise and Storm Surges." *Climatic Change* 106 (4): 567–79.

Emerson, John W., Daniel C. Hillhouse, Tanja Srebotnjak, and Diana Connett. 2011. "Exploring Trade and the Environment: An Empirical Examination of Trade Openness and National Environmental Performance." Yale Center for Environmental Law and Policy, Yale University, New Haven, CT. https://envirocenter.yale.edu/sites/default/files/files/exploring_trade_and_the_environment.pdf.

Fayolle, Virginie, Caroline Fouvet, Vidya Soundarajan, Vandana Nath, Sunil Acharya, Naman Gupta, and Luca Petrarulo. 2019. "Engaging the Private Sector in Financing Adaptation to Climate Change: Learning from Practice." Action on Climate Today Learning Paper, Oxford Policy Management, Oxford, February 2019. http://www.acclimatise.uk.com/wp-content/uploads/2019/02/ACT-Private-Sector-paper_final_web-res.pdf.

Goldstein, Allie, Will R. Turner, Jillian Gladstone, and David Hole. 2018. "The Private Sector's Climate Change Risk and Adaptation Blind Spots." *Nature Climate Change* 9 (1): 18–25.

Hallegatte, Stéphane, Mook Bangalore, Laura Bonzanigo, Marianne Fay, Tamaro Kane, Ulf Narloch, Julie Rozenberg, David Treguer, and Adrien Vogt-Schilb. 2016. *Shock Waves: Managing the Impacts of Climate Change on Poverty. Climate Change and Development.* Washington, DC: World Bank.

Heininen, Lassi, Heather Exner-Pirot, and Joël Plouffe, eds. 2015. *Redefining Arctic Security: Artic Yearbook 2015.* Akureyi: Northern Research Forum.

Nhemachena, Charles, and Rashid Hassan. 2007. "Micro-Level Analysis of Farmers' Adaptation to Climate Change in Southern Africa." IFPRI Discussion Paper, International Food Policy Research Institute, Washington, DC.

Ouraich, Ismail, Hasan Dudu, Wallace E. Tyner, and Erol H. Cakmak. 2019. "Agriculture, Trade, and Climate Change Adaptation: A Global CGE Analysis for Morocco and Turkey." *Journal of North African Studies* 24 (6): 961–91. doi: 10.1080/13629387.2018.1463847.

Pauw, Karl, James Thurlow, and Dirk van Seventer. 2010. "Drought and Floods in Malawi: Assessing the Economy-wide Effects." IFPRI Discussion Paper 00962, International Food Policy Research Institute, Washington, DC. https://www.preventionweb.net/files/13792 _ifpridp009621.pdf.

Shakoor, Usman, Abdul Saboor, Ikram Ali, and A. Q. Mohsin. 2011. "Impact of Climate Change on Agriculture: Empirical Evidence from the Arid Region." *Pakistan Journal of Agricultural Sciences* 48 (4): 327–33. https://www.pakjas.com.pk/papers/1966.pdf.

Shiryaevskaya, Ana, Laura Millan Lombrana, and Olga Tanas. 2020. "Longest Arctic Shipping Season Tops Off a Year of Climate Disasters." *Bloomberg*, December 13. https://gcaptain .com/longest-arctic-shipping-season-tops-off-a-year-of-climate-disaste.

Stevens, Tilele, and Kaveh Madani. 2016. "Future Climate Impacts on Maize Farming and Food Security in Malawi." *Scientific Reports* 6: 36241. doi: 10.1038/srep36241.

WMO (World Meteorological Organization). 2021a. "2020 Was One of Three Warmest Years on Record." Press release, January 15. https://public.wmo.int/en/media/press-release /2020-was-one-of-three-warmest-years-record.

WMO (World Meteorological Organization). 2021b. WMO Atlas of Mortality and Economic Losses from Weather, Climate and Water Extremes (1970–2019). WMO-No. 1267. Geneva: WMO. https://library.wmo.int/doc_num.php?explnum_id=10769.

2

Low- and Middle-Income Countries, Carbon Emissions, and Trade

Trade, global value chains, and emissions

The suggestion that increased trade automatically increases greenhouse gas emissions is popular but not squarely true, as increased trade over time in the right types of goods and services, along with complementary regulations, can benefit the environment. The Environmental Kuznets Curve (EKC) captures this relationship perfectly. More specifically, the EKC hypothesis is often used to explain the phenomenon that environmental degradation occurs with increasing economic growth until the country attains middle-income status, after which the environmental impacts start to decline.

This relationship often happens through three independent effects on greenhouse gas emissions—scale, composition, and technique. The World Trade Organization (WTO) defines the "scale" effect as the change in the amount of emissions attributed to the increased output or economic activity resulting from freer trade; the "composition" effect refers to the change in the mix of a country's production, in the wake of trade liberalization, toward those products where it has a comparative advantage; and the "technique" effect alludes to the changes (mainly improvements) in energy efficiency derived from opening trade, which reduces the amount of greenhouse gas emissions from the production of goods and services.

Notably, environmental economists have debated the validity of the EKC hypothesis, with some doubting the U-curve relationship between economic growth and environmental degradation (Das Neves Almeida et al. 2017; Özokcu and Özdemir 2017). However, other researchers have reinforced this theory (Hanif et al. 2019; Ulucak and Bilgili 2018, among others). In fact, in examining the relationship between economic development and environmental degradation based on the EKC, Maneejuk et al. (2020) find that the EKC hypothesis is valid in 3 out of the 8 international economic communities covering 44 countries across the world—namely, the European Union (EU), the G-7, and the Organisation for Economic Co-operation and Development (OECD).

Although the growth of trade and integration into global value chains has slowed since the financial crisis of 2008, countries that are deeply plugged into global value chains experience greater economic benefits; global shocks threaten this kind of integration. Over the past two decades, structural changes occurring in the global economy have reshaped global production and international trade, leading to the rise of global value chains. An estimated 70 percent of international trade flows are plugged into global value chains today. Trade has grown at a slower rate, and the growth of global value chains has slowed as well, mainly due to increasing nationalistic tendencies, an uptake in digitalization, and country-specific concerns about sustainability (Zhan, Casella, and Bolwijn 2020). Moreover, the past two years have witnessed unprecedented global shocks from deepening trade tensions related to the COVID-19 pandemic. These shocks have disrupted global value chains and led to calls for the public and private sectors to rethink their policies. The pandemic has revealed the extent to which supply and value chains can transmit a crisis across countries.

While world trade shows signs of rebounding, recovery is still uncertain and could be disrupted by ongoing pandemic effects, so it is important to make these global value chains sustainable and ensure that growth is resilient to external shocks. In addition, the pandemic has led to a shortage of production factors such as labor and capital, slowing down production in large, coronavirus-affected economies such as China, Europe, and the United States, which are at the center of global manufacturing and trade networks. The slowdown in these countries' production inevitably leads to significant supply-chain interruptions (Lenzen et al. 2020), causing worldwide reductions in production and consumption (Cui et al. 2020). In addition, current trade is likely to fall more steeply in sectors characterized by complex value-chain links, particularly in electronics and automotive products and in services trade, which have already suffered a 23 percent decline. Given these trends, the WTO estimates a 5.3 percent decline in the volume of world merchandise trade in 2020, followed by an 8.0 percent rise in 2021 (WTO 2021). Clearly, if a health disaster can be transmitted along the chains, a climate change crisis could follow the same path. Studies have already shown that emissions embodied in production from one country are often transferred to another.

Given the transfer of emissions from low- and middle-income to high-income countries along global value chains, it is important to understand the country-specific territorial emissions embedded in exports. Globally, according to the latest estimates, carbon dioxide (CO_2) emissions associated with the production and distribution of traded goods and services (8 billion tons) constitute a quarter of total global emissions (32 billion tons) (Banque de France 2020). Additionally, high-income nations collectively have higher *consumption-based emissions* (the United States imports 15 percent of the 8 billion tons for consumption) than *territory-based emissions*, meaning that they are net importers of emissions and thus benefit from carbon-intensive production abroad (Arto and Dietzenbacher 2014). These effects are growing over time, and the net transfer of emissions (production minus consumption) via international trade from high-income to low- and middle-income countries increased by a factor of four between 1990 and the 2008 global financial crisis, exceeding the emissions reductions obtained within the Kyoto Protocol (Peters et al. 2011).

Policies aimed at reducing CO_2 emissions can increase a country's participation in global value chains, but the environmental effects of trade will depend on complementary policies and regulations. For example, Wu, Guisheng, and Baogui (2020) find that causality between participation in global value chains and CO_2 emissions has different aspects at the global and regional levels. At the global level, a feedback causal relationship exists between participation in global value chains and CO_2 emissions. Environmental policies aimed at reducing CO_2 emissions will boost participation in global value chains, while policies such as trade-related industrial innovation policies will cause environmental degradation. The causality from participation in global value chains to CO_2 emissions is unidirectional. Participation in global value chains is raising CO_2 emissions in the Asia-Pacific region, indicating that global-value-chain policies could lead to environmental damage. However, in Sub-Saharan Africa, environmental policies are encouraging participation in global value chains.

Therefore, to promote participation in global value chains and reduce emissions, trade policies should consider technological innovation that reduces traditional energy consumption and increases renewable energy consumption. Environmental effects could arise from a combination of real income effects that will *increase* damages, an efficiency effect that will *reduce* damages, and leakage or externality effects that may *increase or decrease* damages. Consequently, understanding the emissions structure of low- and middle-income countries and identifying appropriate policies for increasing their participation in global value chains while simultaneously leading to positive environmental outcomes are critical.

Understanding emissions from the developing world

Profile of the emerging emitters

Low- and middle-income countries have been carbonizing increasingly in recent years, collectively emerging as the world's third top emitter of emissions, after China and the United States. These increasingly carbonizing countries are called "emerging emitters." Figure 2.1 compares the percentage changes over 2010–18 in annual CO_2 emissions and gross domestic product (GDP) among the 59 emerging emitters; map 2.1 shows their GDP per capita and annual CO_2 emissions growth rate.[1] The average annual growth rate of emissions of the 59 emerging emitters was 6.2 percent in 2010–18—much higher than the 2.0 percent worldwide average and higher than the 4.6 percent annual growth rate of these same countries' GDP, reflecting the rising carbonization of their economies. Located in Africa, Asia, and Latin America, individually these countries emitted between 0.7 million and 542.9 million tons of CO_2 in 2018 (bounded by Eritrea and Indonesia, respectively). However, taken together, the countries' emissions grew by 40.7 percent in the period under study—from 2.7 gigatons to 3.8 gigatons of CO_2. Moreover, the 1.1 gigaton increase in emissions accounts for 38.9 percent of the global increase in emissions over the period.

Figure 2.2 compares these same figures with those for China, India, and the United States over the period 2010–18. By comparison, the CO_2 emissions of China, the United States, and India amounted to 9.6 gigatons, 4.9 gigatons, and 2.3 gigatons, respectively, in 2018. The aggregated GDP of emerging emitters in 2018 (in 2010 constant US dollars) amounted to US$8.2 trillion, compared to the 2018 GDP for China, India, and the United States of US$10.9 trillion, US$2.8 trillion, and US$17.9 trillion, respectively. The annual growth of CO_2 emissions of China, India, and the United States was 2.5 percent, 4.9 percent, and −1.0 percent, respectively. The annual

FIGURE 2.1 Changes in Annual CO$_2$ Emissions and GDP of the 59 Emerging Emitters, 2010–18

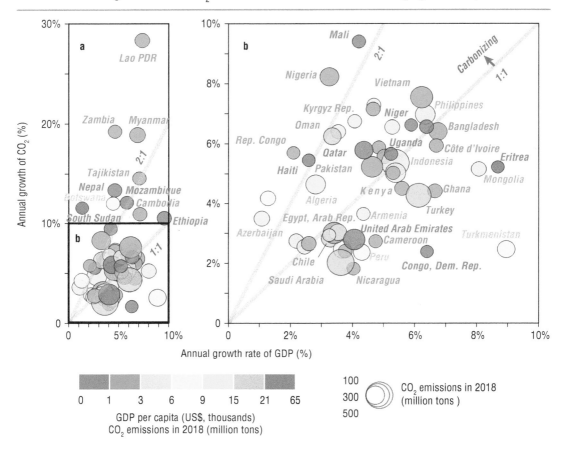

Source: Cui et al. 2020.

GDP growth rates of the entire world (average), China, India, and the United States were 3.14 percent, 7.5 percent, 6.7 percent, and 2.3 percent, respectively.

Emerging emitters have significantly lower levels of GDP per capita than the world average as well as higher levels of poverty. While they comprise countries in development categories ranging from the lowest-income countries to economies in transition, in most cases, their GDP per capita is substantially lower than the global average (53 countries have GDP per capita below US$11,000 in constant 2010 US dollars). In 2017, 698 million people in these countries were living in absolute poverty—that is, earning less than US$1.90 per day in purchasing power parity (PPP) value. This figure represents 9.3 percent of the global population. Among the 59 emerging emitters, emissions grew faster than GDP in 34 countries (58 percent) and twice as fast as GDP in 12 countries (20 percent). In 25 other countries (42 percent), economic growth outstripped emissions growth, corresponding to decreasing carbon intensity.

MAP 2.1 Rate of Growth of CO_2 Emissions, 2010–18, and GDP per Capita

Source: World Bank.
Note: CO_2 = carbon dioxide.

FIGURE 2.2 CO_2 Emissions and GDP Growth of 59 Emerging Emitters, China, India, and the United States, 2010–18

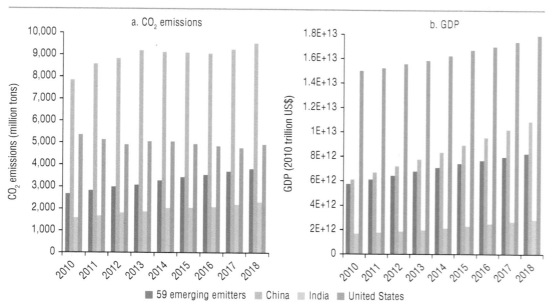

Source: Cui et al. 2020.
Note: CO_2 = carbon dioxide.

Drivers of recent emission surges

Across all 59 emerging emitters, higher GDP per capita and population growth have been the most important drivers of emissions growth. Figure 2.3 shows the two main drivers and two main inhibitors of the rise in emissions between 2010 and 2018 for 20 countries in Africa, Asia, and Latin America. An increase in GDP per capita was the foremost driver of emissions increases in 44 percent of the countries, including Colombia, Ethiopia, and Vietnam. In the next 29 percent of the countries, including Lebanon and Uganda, population growth was the most significant driver. Following closely behind these socioeconomic factors were increases in the use of a particular fossil fuel, with increases in the use of either oil or coal as the most influential factors of emissions increases in 14 percent of the 59 emerging emitters, including Guatemala, Haiti, the Kyrgyz Republic, Myanmar, and Sudan. Energy intensity was one of the top two drivers of emissions growth in 12 percent of the countries, including Algeria and the Lao People's Democratic Republic.

A decline in energy intensity was the most critical driver of emissions reductions. A rise in the CO_2 emissions intensity of energy use contributed to emissions growth the most in 5 percent of the countries, including Botswana, Nepal, and Nicaragua. By comparison, a decline in energy intensity was the most influential driver of emissions reduction in a third (32 percent) of the countries, including Ethiopia, Mongolia, Uganda, and United Arab Emirates, followed by a fall in the CO_2 emissions intensity of energy use in 20 percent of the countries, including Haiti, Peru, and Sudan, a smaller share of industrial value added in 15 percent of the countries, especially in Latin America and in some Asian countries, and a declining share of oil use in 15 percent of the countries, including Botswana and Nepal.

Implications for global climate efforts and the role of trade policy

Emerging emitters collectively have contributed extremely little to the overall stock of CO_2 in the atmosphere, but they have come to the forefront of the growth of CO_2 emissions over the past decade and will likely increasingly do so. These emissions will be influenced by strong and sustained economic growth, which is crucial for poverty reduction, and by population growth. Moreover, heavy consumption of carbon energy will continue to drive significant emissions growth from these countries. The COVID-19 pandemic has pushed more people into poverty, and the current dependence on traditional fossil fuels is likely to result in sizable carbon emissions. While COVID-related shutdowns are expected to reduce emissions in the next few years, countries will, regardless of the severity of the lockdowns, quickly return to a trajectory whereby emissions by 2040 will substantially exceed those in published scenarios that limit global warming to 2°C. As such, there is urgency to revive growth quickly using tools that facilitate sustainable growth.

These countries are confronting the massive challenges of achieving inclusive economic development, contributing to climate change mitigation, and adapting to rising global temperatures, changing precipitation patterns, and more extreme weather events. Indeed, these emerging emitters are the most vulnerable and least prepared to adapt to climate change. What is more, climate change will undermine their ability to reduce poverty because it will constrain their productivity growth, especially in

FIGURE 2.3 Countries with Surging Emissions and Their Drivers, by Region, 2010–18

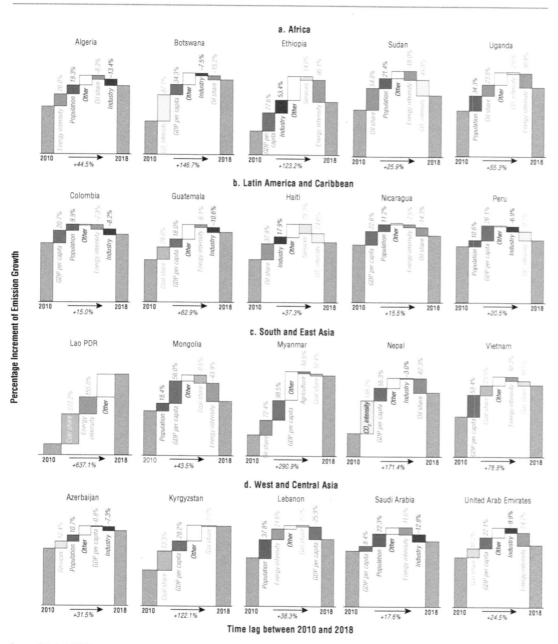

Source: Cui et al. 2020.

Note: Emissions are expressed in millions of tons. The waterfalls show the drivers of emissions growth from 2010 to 2018, including factors increasing consumption (population, GDP per capita), factors affecting economic structure (industrial structure, including share of value added of primary, secondary, and tertiary industry and GDP energy intensity), and factors affecting carbon intensity (energy structure, including share of consumption of coal, oil, natural gas, and other fuels and CO_2 emission intensity of energy). The total increment for each country is reflected at the base of the graph, e.g., Uganda's emissions grew by 55.3 percent, mainly driven by population growth, between 2010 and 2018. CO_2 = carbon dioxide.

agriculture, and will require scarce resources to be redirected toward adaptation. Costinot, Donaldson, and Smith (2016), for example, compute that the impact of climate change on agricultural productivity alone will result in a decline in welfare equivalent to almost 4 percent of GDP in Uganda and more than 6.5 percent of GDP in Vietnam. This scenario assumes that the patterns of trade and production will adjust to dampen the impact. If adjustment is constrained, losses could amount to more than 7.5 percent of GDP in Uganda and more than 11 percent in Vietnam.

In order to limit global warming to 2°C above preindustrial levels, the world will have to reduce emissions by 25 percent with respect to 2018 levels—an uphill task that requires unprecedented efforts from all countries. For this reason, adaptation will be critical. The emerging emitters are highly diverse in the absolute level of national CO_2 emissions, the relationship between GDP growth and increases in CO_2 emissions, the drivers of emissions growth, the response to the COVID pandemic, and the impact of alternative post-COVID pathways. Many of these countries are making commendable strides in enhancing the ambition of their nationally determined contributions under the Paris Agreement. However, in the post-COVID era, the outcomes from different pathways could lead to a difference of more than 1 gigaton in emissions from these countries. As many of these countries are already feeling the adverse effects of climate change and dealing with changing comparative advantages, adaptation mechanisms need to be at the forefront of the discussions.

A global move toward a "low-carbon lifestyle" would entail significant changes in consumption and in how products are made. Low-carbon technologies are crucial to limiting the surge in emissions. The analysis shows that the adoption of low-carbon technologies can considerably influence future reductions in emissions—with early application of carbon capture and storage and renewable energy in the power sector and with electric vehicles replacing oil-fueled cars, the emerging emitters could reduce emissions by 600 metric tons of CO_2 equivalent by 2040.[2] However, while the adoption of new, low-carbon technologies can help to reduce the emissions of the emerging emitters, new technologies alone will not enable them to follow a sustainable pathway in line with the international consensus on the limits of global warming.

Removing barriers to trade in the products that can support the move to a low-carbon future and facilitating the sharing of knowledge on how to implement the transition can be important steps to support the efforts of low- and middle-income countries to reduce emissions. The challenge for the global community is to facilitate these economic transformations in ways that support sustained growth and poverty reduction. Doing so requires understanding the climate and development impacts of the policies (especially trade policies) being put forward as necessary to achieve global warming objectives. These policies include imposing domestic carbon taxes (PMR 2017) and carbon border tax adjustments;[3] removing subsidies to fossil fuel production and consumption; reducing tariffs on trade in green goods; ensuring consistency between trade taxes on dirty and clean goods;[4] and improving access to the technologies, finance, and knowledge necessary to support global adoption of new, low-carbon sources of energy and less energy-intensive production.

More generally, simultaneously addressing the challenges of ending extreme poverty, achieving inclusive growth throughout the world, and meeting climate goals will require cooperative solutions that consider both the development needs and emission realities of low- and middle-income countries. More specifically, while countries at all income levels refer to renewable energy, low- and middle-income economies often identify it as a priority. These emerging emitters need support from the global community to work toward achieving their commitments, especially in the form of large-scale and effective technology transfer, financing, and capacity strengthening. Further analysis can help to identify the coordinated policy measures that will allow countries to achieve their objectives regarding poverty reduction, structural transformation, and adaptation to climate change, while stabilizing their emissions and contributing to meeting internationally agreed-on climate targets.

Policy makers have paid little attention to trade measures as a tool for environmental policy, and this situation needs to change. According to a 2017 study of trade commitments undertaken in response to the Paris Agreement, "The major emitters and net exporters of carbon do not put a strong focus on trade or trade-related measures" (Brandi 2017). However, several trade policies are related to climate, and a few are highlighted in this section, with an emphasis on tariffs, as restructuring tariffs could be the necessary first step for most governments in facilitating greener trade.

Current tariff structures and nontariff barriers are biased toward dirty industries, thus implicitly subsidizing CO_2 emissions.[5] Shapiro (2020) finds that in most countries the rates of tariffs and nontariff barriers—for both cooperative and noncooperative tariffs and over several years—are substantially higher on clean than on dirty goods. Tariffs and nontariff barriers differ for clean and dirty industries because industries tend to be well organized, while final consumers generally are not. As a result, countries impose higher tariffs and nontariff barriers on downstream (clean) goods and lower tariffs and nontariff barriers on upstream (dirty) goods. In fact, firms often lobby for high protection for their own outputs but low protection for their intermediate inputs. This skewed bias, resulting from trade policy, creates an implicit subsidy for CO_2 generation. An industry's "dirtiness" in this analysis is defined by the total amount of CO_2 emitted to produce a dollar of output. This implicit subsidy totals US$550 billion to US$800 billion per year, significantly higher than the direct global subsidies for fossil fuel consumption, estimated at about US$530 billion per year.

Leveling the playing field by imposing similar tariffs and nontariff barriers on clean and dirty industries would have significant positive effects. Using a general equilibrium model, Shapiro (2020) postulates that if countries impose similar tariffs and nontariff barriers on clean and dirty industries, global CO_2 emissions would fall, while global real income would remain unchanged or increase slightly. Further, and with significant effects, these changes in global CO_2 emissions are of comparable scale to the estimated impacts of some of the world's largest actual or proposed climate change policies.

Evidence suggests that cutting tariffs in dirty sectors, without appropriate carbon policies, leads to higher emissions and more environmental pollution. If environmental policies do not account for the emissions embodied in imports, global emissions are likely to rise (Kanemoto et al. 2014). Islam, Kanemoto, and Managi (2019) find that a reduction in tariff barriers facilitates the relocation of factories to countries with less stringent environmental regulations. The carbon footprint of those emissions from low- and medium-income countries to high-income countries has grown rapidly over the past 30 years through international trade. However, almost all countries maintain their tariff barriers, and these tariffs limit the potential to increase CO_2 emission transfers. The findings reveal that a 1 percent tariff cut by G-20 countries for mining gas, manufactured machinery, metal, and other mining imports would result in 2,779 tons, 1,747 tons, 1,453 tons, and, 1,018 tons of CO_2 emissions, respectively. Additionally, a tariff cut would increase the embodied CO_2 emissions significantly for most of the manufacturing and mining sectors. He and Huang (2020) find that reducing import tariffs on final goods and intermediate inputs in the Central America Free Trade Agreement (CAFTA) could reduce firms' pollution emissions through both the "technique effect" and the "composition effect." Thus, it is essential to make full use of both technique and composition effects to reduce emissions by reducing import tariffs in CAFTA.

Trade agreements have traditionally described environmental regulations, but rarely address restructuring tariffs to promote cleaner goods or removing nontariff barriers to facilitate greener trade. The World Bank's Deep Trade Agreement database 2.0 reveals that of all the trade agreements globally, the EU's trade agreements have attempted to include environmental provisions in the most significant way, covering issues of institutions, cooperation, and welfare and including an enforcement mechanism. However, Shapiro (2020) finds that these agreements typically describe domestic environmental regulations or monitoring investments, but not patterns of tariffs and nontariff barriers. Many of these investments merely seek to prevent the relocation of dirty industries by barring the use of weak domestic environmental policies to lure dirty production across borders. Governments need to delineate the types of trade policies that affect the environment so that appropriate amendments can be made.

A tariff restructuring biased toward lower duties for high-technology green sectors would have significant payoffs for low- and middle-income countries, both in terms of emissions and in terms of poverty rates (box 2.1). Taking the example of Bangladesh, a green-trade scenario could remove 45 metric tons of CO_2 equivalent

---

BOX 2.1 Modeling Postpandemic Impacts under Different Trade Scenarios

This study defines three scenarios for trade patterns in the postpandemic era, based on the default COVID-19 scenario that the pandemic will last for three years:

- *Deglobalization*. Import tariff rates on all commodities (except for agricultural products) between all countries are increased by 30 percent. In this scenario, the competitiveness of domestic products increases, while the competitiveness of imported products decreases. The supply chain becomes more dependent on domestic products.
- *Free trade*. Import tariff rates on all commodities (except for agricultural products) between all countries are set to 0. In this scenario, all countries enjoy free trade.
- *Green trade*. Import tariff rates on products from carbon-intensive commodities (that is, light and heavy manufacturing, transportation equipment industries) between all countries are increased by 30 percent, and import tariff rates on products from high-tech industries between all countries are set to 0.

Impact of trade scenarios on emissions

The emissions trajectory and changes in energy structure under different trade patterns were estimated using a computable general equilibrium model that assesses carbon dioxide (CO_2) emissions under different trade scenarios and energy mix projections from the Greenhouse Gas–Air Pollution Interactions and Synergies (GAINS) model.

In selected low-income countries, results show that, although fossil fuels will still constitute the highest share of the 2040 energy mix, promoting greener pathways would significantly offset the rapid increment in emissions, which is inevitably brought about by a booming economy. Specifically, a green-trade scenario in renewable energies such as wind and solar would contribute significantly to a country's emissions removal effort. In all countries, the reduction in emissions is significantly higher in the green-trade scenario than in the business-as-usual trajectory with no COVID-19.

(Box continues next page)

BOX 2.1 Modeling Postpandemic Impacts under Different Trade Scenarios (*Continued*)

Figure B2.1.1 shows the results of five scenarios (with COVID, no COVID, green trade, free trade, and deglobalization) for the evolution of CO_2 emissions. Numbers marked on the left side of each line chart represent the maximum and minimum CO_2 emissions of the five scenarios in 2040, respectively. To note, the International Energy Agency excludes biomass from its calculations of CO_2 emissions. Therefore, biomass energy is included in the description of the current state of national energy structure but is neglected in the simulation of future emission and energy structure scenarios.

FIGURE B2.1.1 CO_2 Emissions in Selected Countries in the Postpandemic Era under Different Trade Pattern Scenarios, 2019–40

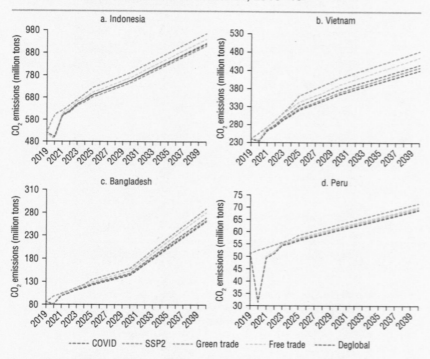

Sources: AghaKouchak et al. 2020; Hu et al. 2021.
Note: COVID = with COVID-19 scenario; Deglobal = deglobalization scenario; Free trade = free-trade scenario; Green trade = green-trade scenario; SSP2 = business-as-usual scenario.

Impact of trade scenarios on poverty alleviation in low-income countries
Linking a global economic model (Global Trade Analysis Project [GTAP] model) to a micro household survey data set makes it possible to assess the impact of COVID-19 and the potential impact of deglobalization in the postpandemic era on economic growth and achievement of the United Nations Sustainable Development Goal of eradicating extreme poverty. Results show that the capacity to alleviate poverty and ability to adapt to the impact of the COVID-19 crisis varies greatly among regions, especially for low-income countries. South American countries have a low poverty rate and a small population base; as such, the rate of decline in the poverty rate is relatively small.

Specifically, when compared to deglobalization scenarios, free trade also contributes to poverty reduction, especially for people who are struggling under extreme poverty (figure B2.1.2). The panels show the poverty rate at different poverty lines for the five scenarios. Projections are available for 85 countries.

(Box continues next page)

BOX 2.1 Modeling Postpandemic Impacts under Different Trade Scenarios (*Continued*)

FIGURE B2.1.2 Poverty Rate in Selected Countries in the Postpandemic Era under Different Trade Pattern Scenarios, 2024–50

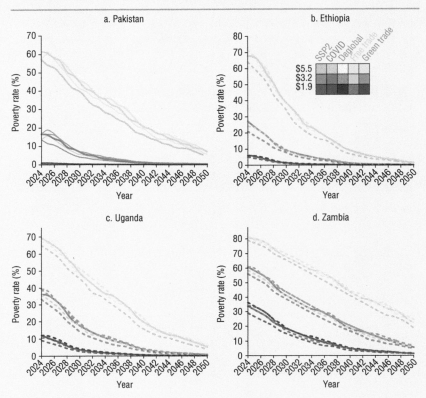

Sources: AghaKouchak et al. 2020; Hu et al. 2021.
Note: COVID = with COVID-19 scenario; Deglobal = deglobalization scenario; Free trade = free-trade scenario; Green trade = green-trade scenario; SSP2 = business-as-usual scenario.

Taking Ethiopia as an example, 18.3 percent (< US$1.90 purchasing power parity [PPP] per day), 37.6 percent (US$1.90–$3.20 PPP per day), and 32.6 percent (US$3.20–US$5.50 PPP per day) of the total population were living below these poverty lines in 2010. Due to the pandemic's impact, the extreme poverty rate in Ethiopia will remain at 18.3 percent in 2021 in a default scenario but will decline to 7.9 percent in 2024.

(accumulated value) of emissions by 2040, equal to 53 percent of national emissions in 2019. Notably, a free-trade scenario without a positive bias toward greener high-technology goods would increase emissions by 6.86 metric tons of CO_2 equivalent. Facilitating trade for these types of products is critical. In addition, a deglobalization reaction to the COVID-19 pandemic would exacerbate the already worsening poverty levels, increasing globally to 17 percent (US$1.90–US$3.20 PPP per day) by 2040 from only 9.2 percent in 2017. The reduction in poverty is most significant under a free-trade scenario—dropping to 2 percent (US$3.20–US$5.50 PPP per day) (Hu et al. 2021).

Examining agriculture as one of the main trade-related sectors affecting emissions from the developing world

The export structure of most low- and middle-income countries is based on agriculture, signaling agriculture's critical importance for jobs, income, poverty reduction, and government revenue. However, the Intergovernmental Panel on Climate Change (IPCC) estimates that land-use change—for example, conversion of forest into agricultural land—adds a net 1.6 ± 0.8 gigaton of carbon per year to the atmosphere, which is similar to a quarter of emissions from fossil fuel combustion and cement production (Watson et al. 2000). The expansion of large-scale commercial agriculture is often viewed as the culprit, but the collective emissions from subsistence farmers and outgrowers[6] also contribute significantly. Moreover, while agriculture exacerbates climate change (through deforestation and in other ways), it also suffers from the adverse effects of climate change—among others, growing water scarcity. This section examines the problem and provides suggestions on how trade can help to increase agricultural output sustainably while reducing land-use change.

Impact of trade on land-use change and emissions, especially in low-income African countries

Since the advent of agriculture, natural forests and habitats have been cleared to engage in crop and animal production, but these changes in land use are contributing to growing emissions. In more recent periods, clearing for industrial activities has also played a role, but not at commensurate levels. The United Nations Climate Change Secretariat defines land use, land-use change, and forestry (LULUCF), also referred to as forestry and other land use, as "a greenhouse gas inventory sector that covers emissions and removals of GHGs [greenhouse gases] resulting from direct human-induced land use such as settlements and commercial uses, land-use change, and forestry activities."[7] The impacts of LULUCF on climate are direct—changing the global carbon cycle. LULUCF activities either add CO_2 to the atmosphere or remove it, thus bringing about changes in biodiversity and climate patterns.

Since international trade involves mainly commodities produced where resources are most abundant, several countries clear forests to enable productive activities destined for export. On average, the harvest of one-fifth of global cropland area was destined for export in the 2000s, and almost all growth in cropland area was for internationally traded crops (Kastner, Erb, and Haberl 2014). Demand for the final and intermediate products made with forest-risk commodities is global, but production and associated land-use change are geographically decoupled from the associated demand (Henders, Persson, and Kastner 2015).

Commodities whose production entails deforestation vary between regions and countries; in the case of Africa, they are largely livestock meat and some cereals. Specifically, production of cattle meat contributes just over a quarter, and the remainder is from the production of a diverse mix of other cereals, roots and tubers, pulses, and other oilseeds (Pendrill et al. 2019). In Latin America, the production of cattle meat accounts for more than 60 percent of embodied deforestation. In Asia and Pacific, the production of palm oil and forestry products each accounts for a third of embodied deforestation. For example, in Argentina, Brazil, Indonesia, and Malaysia, the production of soybeans and palm oil during the 1990–2014 period led to a forest loss of more than 60 million hectares.

The problem: Increasing deforestation caused by fuel agricultural exports despite suboptimal productivity per acreage

Tree cover loss has been significant in Africa, with the remaining primary forest cover mainly in the Democratic Republic of Congo and distributed sparsely in parts of West Africa and East Africa. Between 2001 and 2019, tree cover loss accelerated in Africa. The Democratic Republic of Congo experienced the greatest loss, ranking sixth in the world in terms of forest cover loss, losing 14.6 million hectares over the past two decades. The Democratic Republic of Congo is followed by Madagascar (3.89 million hectares) and Mozambique (3.29 million hectares), Côte d'Ivoire (3.03 million hectares), and Tanzania (2.51 million hectares). (The Russian Federation had the highest relative tree cover loss in the world, equivalent to 64.0 million hectares, which represented 8.4 percent of tree cover in 2000.) Forests present a significant stock of global carbon, accumulated through the growth of trees and increase in soil carbon. Tampering with primary forests—converting primary to managed forests, illegal logging, and unsustainable forest management—results in greenhouse gas emissions and can have additional physical effects on the regional climate (IPCC 2019).

In the past decade, the value of the poorest countries' oil and gas exports has almost halved, whereas agriculture and textile manufacturing exports have increased gradually (figure 2.4). In 2019 oil and gas extraction exports were US$45.3 billion, down from US$85.1 billion in 2012. Agriculture and textile manufacturing exports

FIGURE 2.4 Categories of Exports from the Poorest Countries to the World (Mirror Data), 2012–19

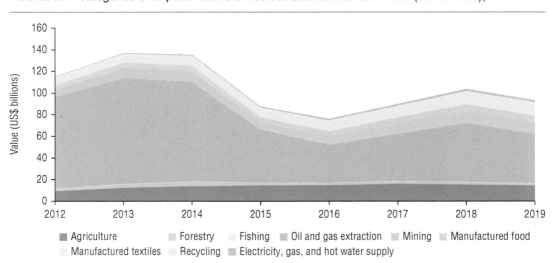

Source: International Trade Statistics (COMTRADE) data.

both increased by about US$5.0 billion, while average forestry exports amounted to US$1.8 billion over the same period. In Sub-Saharan Africa, land is used mostly for agriculture; between 1990 and 2018, agricultural land grew by 4 percent, while forest area declined by almost the same percentage.

Africa is the only region where emissions due to agriculture and related land use are higher than those due to energy. Africa remains an agricultural powerhouse, and recent investments in large-scale commercial farming are having an adverse effect on the environment. By 2013, the value of agricultural production in Africa had tripled compared to levels in 1980; growth was almost identical to or lower than that of South America, but comparable to that of Asia (NEPAD 2013). Between 1990 and 2017, Africa's agricultural emissions ranged from 1.7 million to 1.8 million gigagrams, followed by South America, which saw a substantial reduction over the same period— from 1.8 million to 1.1. million gigagrams. Globally, total emissions not associated with land use have been growing (except for Europe), driven largely by energy, especially in low-income food-deficit countries and South Asia. Industrial processes have also been adding increasingly to CO_2 emissions in these same regions. Europe is the only region exhibiting a decline in both total emissions (excluding land use) and energy.

Although more land is being allocated to agriculture, yields are still very low, signaling that current output may have been achievable with less land-use change. The increase in agricultural output in Africa has been driven by the expansion of cropland rather than an increase in yields. For many crops, yields in Africa remain far below the averages obtained elsewhere in the world. For example, in Sub-Saharan Africa, the area of land dedicated to cereal production has been increasing since 1960, but up to 2017 yields did not grow by a commensurate amount (figure 2.5). More specifically, yields did not even double (growing by a factor of 1.8), while land hectarage almost

FIGURE 2.5 Cereal Production versus Yield on Harvested Land in Sub-Saharan Africa, 1960–2016

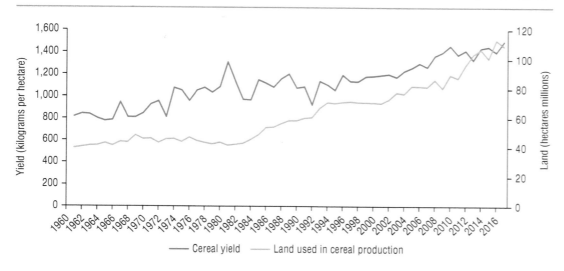

Source: Food and Agriculture Organization, Food and Agriculture Statistics Division (FAOSTAT) database.

tripled (growing a factor of 2.75). Additional analysis by the International Food Policy Research Institute, using Food and Agriculture Organization data, shows that production on the African continent increased fourfold between 2002–05 and 2012–15, while harvested area only increased by a factor of 1.5. Yields doubled in more recent years. However, there is a large regional disparity, with the increase in crop yields and production concentrated in East Africa rather than West Africa. These findings highlight the need to pay attention to regional factors that are constraining or contributing to higher yields.

Moreover, cropland expansion is projected to continue, so innovative solutions to transform agricultural farming while mitigating land-use change are urgently needed. Most agroeconomic models project that total cropland area by 2050 will be 10–25 percent larger than in 2005 (under constant climate). Across all models, most of the cropland expansion will take place in South America and Sub-Saharan Africa. Assédé et al. (2020) and Fenta et al. (2020) add that the most drastic land-use change in the Sudanese and Zambezian regions is the conversion of woodlands to arable land. The question arises how much less land-use change might have been necessary to achieve current levels of output if global average yields had been achieved for the main crops in these regions. With innovative technologies in farming, sustainable techniques, and new cereal strains, for example, hectarage for cereal production need not have tripled, as seen in figure 2.5. This is an avenue where trade can provide the solutions.

How trade (policies) can help to increase agricultural output sustainably and reduce land-use change

Trade liberalization can promote land-use displacement in countries with more established and efficient "environmentally friendly" production systems. Closer examination of trade between Costa Rica and the United States reveals how land use has been spatially redistributed within Costa Rica. Land-use displacement (for cattle production) from Costa Rica to the United States helped to alleviate global environmental pressure. In this example, the United States was a more efficient cattle producer, in that it had a longer agricultural history and an intensive production system. Granted, the initial deforestation to clear land for farming in the United States was not ideal. However, when it came to trade between the two countries, the United States was more efficient at the time and did not need to deforest further. In contrast, Costa Rica was being strained. Jadin, Meyfroidt, and Lambin (2016) find that the contraction of pastures was equivalent to about 80 percent of Costa Rica's reforestation. As pastures were replaced by forests, whose exploitation has been increasingly regulated, Costa Rica has met its domestic demand through production abroad, exporting less meat and importing more wheat, maize, soy products, and rice since the mid-1980s and bovine products since the mid-2000s. Notably, Costa Rica's transition was complemented by enabling policies and regulations on deforestation.

However, this displacement is only positive when it moves into more environmentally friendly sectors—although trade liberalization favors the most productive localization in the sector under consideration, the localization could have smaller or larger environmental impacts. In the positive example above, cattle ranching moved from biodiversity-rich Costa Rica to the United States, not because of lower environmental impacts but because of higher productivity in the meat sector. In Europe, trade liberalization would shift meat production (and feed for cattle) toward Latin America, entailing larger environmental losses. Trade affects the environment through three channels: (1) a *real income effect*, which is detrimental to the environment (lower meat prices will increase demand, damaging the environment); (2) an *efficiency effect*, which is beneficial to the environment (more efficient production can reduce the negative impacts by lowering energy consumption); and (3) *carbon leakage* or *externality effects*, which can be beneficial or detrimental to the environment (positive if production moves from Costa Rica to the United States, negative if it moves from Europe to Brazil).

Trade can foster changes in consumption (and thus demand) to more environmentally friendly products, thus reducing potential land-use change. Changing patterns of demand and consumption is a long-term exercise but necessary to shift production toward more environmentally friendly goods and services. Over the past century, the increasing world population and the shift in global diets toward vegetable oils and animal products have increased the demand for agricultural commodities. To meet this demand, the continuing trend is for forestland to be converted into crop fields or pasture, especially in low- and middle-income countries. This trend is unsustainable. Demand- and consumption-side management is very important because it has the potential to mitigate climate change by reducing emissions from production; switching to consumption of less emission-intensive commodities, for example, plant-based foods; and making land available for CO_2 removal (land that would otherwise have been used for farming). In addition to gains in direct mitigation, lowering meat consumption, primarily of ruminants, and reducing waste further reduce water use, soil degradation, and pressure on forests and land used for feed, potentially freeing up land for mitigation purposes (Tilman and Clark 2014). Several trade policy options are available to "awaken a carbon footprint consciousness in consumption," which are discussed in chapter 5.

Trade measures can promote sustainable agricultural management by fostering technological innovations that can drive up yields while reducing the potential for adverse land-use change. Villoria (2019) concludes that technological progress in Asia and Sub-Saharan Africa would reduce the cropland area in these regions as well as in the rest of the world. Moreover, large-scale application of climate-smart technologies in Africa and Asia could enhance food security. Hertel, Baldos, and Fuglie (2020) find that sluggish growth in farm productivity in Sub-Saharan Africa has brought to the fore the key role of agricultural technology in alleviating future food insecurity and that, toward 2050, virtual technology trade will be the most important vehicle for reducing nonfarm undernutrition in Africa (Hertel, Baldos, and Fuglie 2020). More specifically, given that rice farming produces a significant amount of emissions, disruptive technologies are required. For example, the United Nations Environment Programme has been working with the Shanghai Agrobiological Gene Center to develop rice strains that are drought resistant and do not need to be planted in paddies (UNEP 2021). Generally, technological advancement in the agriculture sector, especially in the making and application of fertilizers, will be necessary to mitigate emissions and adapt to climate change. Countries can increase agricultural productivity in a smart, sustainable manner using existing land—deforestation is not necessary provided yields improve. Moreover, the total area of land that is currently under cultivation may be reduced, paving the way for forestation.

Reducing tariffs on technological goods and liberalizing regulatory policies can facilitate access to agricultural digital technologies and services from advanced economies. Improving digitalization implies that farmers have access to better data, allowing them to make climate-informed decisions, drive up yields, reduce waste, and contribute to poverty reduction in low- and middle-income countries. Along with the large foreign investments being attracted to the poorest countries, which could entail adverse land-use changes, commensurate investments are needed in agricultural research for crop and livestock improvement, agricultural technology transfer, inland capture fisheries, and aquaculture. Additionally, better nitrogen management can help to reduce emissions significantly, depending on soil and weather conditions. Crop farmers need to ensure that the form, type, amount, and timing of nitrogen being applied will not result in significant losses because of denitrification, volatilization, or leaching (Yara International ASA 2021). Further, trade barriers should not impair the movement of agricultural specialists and related professionals, which would hamper the exchange of knowledge and capacity building of farmers.

Land-use change has the potential to affect neighboring countries adversely, especially agricultural production, so regional solutions are necessary. For example, the Congo Basin is home to 80 million people, and the rain forest plays a role in regulating rainfall patterns across other parts of the continent as well. But with increasing losses of forest cover, nearby areas such as the Horn of Africa—for instance, Ethiopia and Somalia—have recently been experiencing droughts. Other factors are probably at play, such as El Niño and climate change, but deforestation within and adjacent to these countries is significant. Country-specific efforts are necessary but not sufficient. For example, South Africa is exploring its potential in green goods (an integrated market for greener technologies, including seeds and fertilizers) and services (movement of agricultural specialists who can help to improve land management).

However, regional liberalization efforts, such as the African Continental Free Trade Area (AfCFTA), can act as an institutional anchor to lock in some of these country-specific efforts that are aligned with fostering sustainable growth. Initially, intra-AfCFTA trade will involve mainly agricultural goods and services. However, agriculture is highly vulnerable to climate change, as higher temperatures will result in lower yields, higher prevalence of diseases, and extreme events such as droughts and flooding. Agriculture also uses huge amounts of water, which is becoming scarcer. Thus, for AfCFTA to be effective, it needs to promote sustainable trade, enabling businesses to adapt effectively to climate change, while minimizing the impacts on the environment.

Environmental provisions in trade agreements can be effective in improving environmental welfare, but need to be specific and legally binding. Recent research shows that countries with stringent environmental regulations particularly benefit from greener trade, enhanced by environmental provisions in preferential trade agreements. Regarding efficacy, Abman, Lundberg, and Ruta (2021) find that the inclusion of deforestation provisions in trade agreements reduced forest loss by 7,571 square kilometers from 1960 to 2020, the effects being most pronounced in ecologically sensitive areas. These provisions limited the expansion of agricultural land but not total production, indicating that agricultural intensification on existing land may still have occurred. Environmental provisions are becoming more diverse and extensive but, for most low- and middle-income countries, provisions lack specificity. The Comprehensive Economic and Trade Agreement between Canada and the EU is a great example of a climate-friendly agreement, with specific provisions (Brandi et al. 2020). As for international forums, the Kyoto Protocol on land use needs to be revised and updated because it requires further clarification and practical, effective implementation methodologies if the potential benefits from land management are to be realized. Countries also need to deepen the implementation of sustainable land management practices embodied in several international conventions, as these provisions can help to attenuate the socioeconomic and environmental impacts of agricultural trade liberalization.

Conclusions

Emerging emitters collectively have contributed extremely little to the overall stock of CO_2 in the atmosphere, but they have moved to the forefront of the growth of CO_2 emissions over the past decade and will likely increasingly do so. These countries are confronting the massive challenges of achieving inclusive economic development, contributing to climate change mitigation, and adapting to rising global temperatures, changing precipitation patterns, and more extreme weather events. To limit global warming to 2°C above preindustrial levels, the world needs to reduce emissions by 25 percent with respect to 2018 levels; emerging emitters have a significant role to play in achieving this level.

Although more land is being allocated to agriculture, yields are still very low, signaling that current output may have been achievable with less land-use change. The following are some important considerations:

- Trade-induced land-use displacement can have positive effects—with global environmental benefits.

- Trade policy options are available to influence patterns of consumption and demand—"climate change consciousness."

- Trade measures can promote sustainable agricultural management by facilitating
  - Access to digital technologies from advanced economies and improved seed varieties
  - Transfer of knowledge and expertise on improving yields
  - Access to quality fertilizers that can boost farmer uptake—better regulation, not trade restrictions.

- To minimize the adverse impacts of trade liberalization and maximize its positive impacts for sustainable land management, two land degradation issues need to be addressed: expansion of agriculture for export and marginalization of smaller farmers.

- The impacts of land-use change are not constrained by borders and thus require regional solutions.

- Trade agreements need to use specific, legally binding language in all climate-related provisions for any change to occur.

Removing barriers to trade in the products that can support the move to a low-carbon future and facilitating knowledge sharing on how to implement the low-carbon transition can significantly support low- and middle-income countries' efforts to reduce emissions. A global move toward a "low-carbon lifestyle" would entail significant changes in the overall consumption mix and in how products are made. More generally, simultaneously addressing the challenges of ending extreme poverty, achieving inclusive growth globally, and meeting climate goals will require cooperative solutions that consider both the development needs and the emissions realities of low- and middle-income countries.

Trade policy has the tools needed to shift an economy toward green growth. Trade agreements have traditionally focused on environmental regulations and rarely have addressed the restructuring of tariffs to support cleaner goods or the removal of nontrade barriers to facilitate greener trade. Evidence shows that leveling the playing field by imposing similar tariffs and nontrade barriers on clean and dirty industries will have significant positive effects. Lower tariffs in dirty sectors exacerbate emissions and environmental pollution. Additionally, as the analysis shows, restructuring tariffs to favor high-technology green sectors is highly beneficial, in terms of both lower emissions and lower poverty. Additionally, governments can remove distortionary subsidies and, jointly with the private sector, put in place standards and labeling requirements specifying the volume of carbon emissions embodied in a product. The international community needs to address these issues in an accelerated manner.

Notes

1. See appendix A for the list of the 59 emerging emitters.

2. Carbon capture and storage is the process of capturing waste carbon dioxide, transporting it to a storage site, and depositing it where it will not enter the atmosphere.

3. A carbon tax explicitly puts a price on greenhouse gas emissions or uses a metric based directly on carbon (that is, price per ton of CO_2 equivalent).

4. Shapiro (2020) finds that in most countries, tariffs and nontariff barriers are higher in cleaner sectors than in dirtier sectors, indicating that relatively clean downstream industries tend to face higher levels of protection.

5. Nontariff barriers are obstacles to international trade other than import or export duties, including quotas, embargoes, and sanctions, among others.

6. Outgrowers are farmers who agree to supply a buyer with crops or livestock at some future time and who meet certain requirements; in return, the buyer agrees to make the purchase (sometimes at a preagreed price) and may provide other kinds of support.

7. For the United Nations glossary of climate change acronyms and terms, see https://unfccc .int/process-and-meetings/the-convention/glossary-of-climate-change-acronyms -and-terms#l.

References

Abman, Ryan, Clark Lundberg, and Michele Ruta. 2021. "The Effectiveness of Environmental Provisions in Regional Trade Agreements." Policy Research Working Paper 9601, World Bank, Washington, DC.

AghaKouchak, Amir, Felicia Chiang, Laurie S. Huning, Charlotte A. Love, Iman Mallakpour, Omar Mazdiyasni, Hamed Moftakhari, et al. 2020. "Climate Extremes and Compound Hazards in a Warming World." *Annual Review of Earth and Planetary Sciences* 48 (1): 519–48. https://doi.org/10.1146/annurev-earth-071719-055228.

Arto, Iñaki, and Erik Dietzenbacher. 2014. "Drivers of the Growth in Global Greenhouse Gas Emissions." *Environmental Science & Technology* 48 (10): 5388–94. https://doi.org/10.1021 /es5005347.

Assédé, Eméline Sêssi Pélagie, Akomian Fortuné Azihou, Coert Johannes Geldenhuys, Paxie Wanangwa Chirwa, and Samadori Sorotori Honoré Biaou. 2020. "Sudanian versus Zambezian Woodlands of Africa: Composition, Ecology, Biogeography, and Use." *Acta Oecologica* 107 (August): 103599. https://doi.org/10.1016/j.actao.2020.103599.

Banque de France. 2020. "CO_2 Emissions Embodied in International Trade." *Bulletin de la Banque de France* 228/1, March–April. https://www.banque-france.fr/sites/default /files/medias/documents/820083_bdf228-1_co2_en_v5.pdf.

Brandi, Clara. 2017. *Trade Elements in Countries' Climate Contributions under the Paris Agreement.* Geneva: International Centre for Trade and Sustainable Development. https://ictsd.iisd.org/sites/default/files/research/trade_elements_in_countries_climate _contributions.pdf.

Brandi, Clara, Jakob Schwab, Axel Berger, and Jean-Frédéric Morin. 2020. "Do Environmental Provisions in Trade Agreements Make Exports from Developing Countries Greener?" *World Development* 129 (May): 104899. https://doi.org/10.1016/j.worlddev.2020.104899.

Costinot, Arnaud, Dave Donaldson, and Cory Smith. 2016. "Evolving Comparative Advantage and the Impact of Climate Change in Agricultural Markets: Evidence from 1.7 Million Fields around the World." *Journal of Political Economy* 124 (1): 205–48. https://doi.org/10.1086 /684719.

Cui, Can, Dabo Guan, Daoping Wang, Vicky Chemutai, and Paul Brenton. 2020. "Emerging Emitters and Global Carbon Mitigation Efforts." Working Paper, World Bank, Washington, DC. https://openknowledge.worldbank.org/handle/10986/35845.

Das Neves Almeida, Thiago A., Luís Cruz, Eduardo Barata, and Isabel-María Garcia-Sanchez. 2017. "Economic Growth and Environmental Impacts: An Analysis Based on a Composite Index of Environmental Damage." *Ecological Indicators* 76 (May): 119–30.

Fenta, Ayele Almaw, Atsushi Tsunekawa, Nigussie Haregeweyn, Mitsuru Tsubo, Hiroshi Yasuda, Katsuyuki Shimizu, Takayuki Kawai, et al. 2020. "Cropland Expansion Outweighs the Monetary Effect of Declining Natural Vegetation on Ecosystem Services in Sub-Saharan Africa." *Ecosystem Services* 45 (October): 101154. https://doi.org/10.1016/j.ecoser.2020 .101154.

Hanif, Imran, Syed M. Faraz Raza, Pilar Gago-de-Santos, and Qaiser Abbas. 2019. "Fossil Fuels, Foreign Direct Investment, and Economic Growth Have Triggered CO_2 Emissions in Emerging Asian Economies: Some Empirical Evidence." *Energy* 171 (March 15): 493–501.

He, Ling-Yun, and Geng Huang. 2020. "Tariff Reduction and Environment: Evidence from CAFTA and Chinese Manufacturing Firms." *Sustainability 2020* 12 (5): 1–25. doi: 10.3390/su12052017.

Henders, Sabine, U. Martin Persson, and Thomas Kastner. 2015. "Trading Forests: Land-Use Change, and Carbon Emissions Embodied in Production and Exports of Forest-Risk Commodities." *Environmental Research Letters* 10 (12): 125012.

Hertel, Thomas W., Uris L. C. Baldos, and Keith O. Fuglie. 2020. "Trade in Technology: A Potential Solution to the Food Security Challenges of the 21st Century." NBER Working Paper 27148, National Bureau of Economic Research, Cambridge, MA.

Hu, Yixin, Daoping Wang, Jingwen Huo, Lili Yang, Dabo Guan, Paul Brenton, and Vicky Chemutai. 2021. "Assessing the Economic Impacts of a 'Perfect Storm' of Extreme Weather, Pandemic Control and Deglobalization: A Methodological Construct." Working Paper, World Bank, Washington, DC. http://documents.worldbank.org/curated/en /744851623848784106/Assessing-the-Economic-Impacts-of-a-Perfect-Storm-of -Extreme-Weather-Pandemic-Control-and-Deglobalization-A-Methodological-Construct.

IPCC (Intergovernmental Panel on Climate Change). 2019. *Climate Change and Land: An IPCC Special Report on Climate Change, Desertification, Land Degradation, Sustainable Land Management, Food Security, and Greenhouse Gas Fluxes in Terrestrial Ecosystems: Summary for Policymakers,* edited by P. R. Shukla, J. Skea, E. Calvo Buendia, V. Masson-Delmotte, H.-O. Pörtner, D. C. Roberts, P. Zhai, et al. Geneva: IPCC.

Islam, Moinul, Keiichiro Kanemoto, and Shunsuke Managi. 2019. "Growth Potential for CO_2 Emissions Transfer by Tariff Reduction." *Environmental Research Letters* 14 (2): 024011.

Jadin, Isaline, Patrick Meyfroidt, and Eric F. Lambin. 2016. "International Trade, and Land Use Intensification and Spatial Reorganization Explain Costa Rica's Forest Transition." *Environmental Research Letters* 11 (3): 035005. https://iopscience.iop.org/article/10.1088/1748-9326/11/3/035005.

Kanemoto, Keiichiro, Daniel D. Moran, Manfred Lenzen, and Arne Geschke. 2014. "International Trade Undermines National Emission Reduction Targets: New Evidence from Air Pollution." *Global Environmental Change* 24 (January): 52–59. https://doi.org/10.1016/j.gloenvcha.2013.09.008.

Kastner, Thomas, Karl-Heinz Erb, and Helmut Haberl. 2014. "Rapid Growth in Agricultural Trade: Effects on Global Area Efficiency and the Role of Management." *Environmental Research Letters* 9 (3): 034015.

Lenzen, Manfred, Mengyu Li, Arunima Malik, Francesco Pomponi, Ya-Yen Sun, Thomas Wiedmann, Futu Faturay, et al. 2020. "Global Socio-Economic Losses and Environmental Gains from the Coronavirus Pandemic." *PLoS One* 15 (7): e0235654. doi: 10.1371/journal.pone.0235654.

Maneejuk, Nutnaree, Sutthipat Ratchakom, Paravee Maneejuk, and Woraphon Yamaka. 2020. "Does the Environmental Kuznets Curve Exist? An International Study." *Sustainability 2020* 12 (21): 9117. https://doi.org/10.3390/su12219117.

NEPAD (New Partnership for Africa's Development). 2013. *African Agriculture, Transformation, and Outlook*. Lusaka: NEPAD.

Özokcu, Selin, and Özlem Özdemir. 2017. "Economic Growth, Energy, and Environmental Kuznets Curve." *Reviewable and Sustainable Energy Reviews* 72 (May): 639–47. 10.1016/j.rser.2017.01.059.

Pendrill, Florence, U. Martin Persson, Javier Godar, and Thomas Kastner. 2019. "Deforestation Displaced: Trade in Forest-Risk Commodities and the Prospects for a Global Forest Transition." *Environmental Research Letters* 14 (5): 05500. https://iopscience.iop.org/article/10.1088/1748-9326/ab0d41/pdf.

Peters, Glen P., Jan C. Minx, Christopher L. Weber, and Ottmar Edenhofer. 2011. "Growth in Emission Transfers via International Trade from 1990 to 2008." *Proceedings of the National Academy of Sciences* 108 (21): 8903–08. doi: 10.1073/pnas.1006388108.

PMR (Partnership for Market Readiness). 2017. *Carbon Tax Guide: A Handbook for Policy Makers*. Washington, DC: World Bank.

Shapiro, Joseph S. 2020. "The Environmental Bias of Trade Policy." University of Berkeley, May 2. https://ssrn.com/abstract=3591145.

Tilman, David, and Michael Clark. 2014. "Global Diets Link Environmental Sustainability and Human Health." *Nature* 515 (7528): 518–22. https://doi.org/10.1038/nature13959.

Ulucak, Recep, and Faik Bilgili. 2018. "A Reinvestigation of EKC Model by Ecological Footprint Measurement for High, Middle-, and Low-Income Countries." *Journal of Cleaner Production* 188 (July 1): 144–57.

UNEP (United Nations Environment Programme). 2021. "New Strains of Rice Could Address Climate Change." UNEP, Nairobi. https://www.unep.org/news-and-stories/story/new-strains-rice-could-address-climate-change.

Villoria, Nelson B. 2019. "Technology Spillovers and Land-Use Change: Empirical Evidence from Global Agriculture." *American Journal of Agricultural Economics* 101 (3): 870–93. https://doi.org/10.1093/ajae/aay088.

Watson, Robert T., Ian R. Noble, Bert Bolin, N. H. Ravindranath, David J. Verardo, and David J. Dokken, eds. 2000. *Land Use, Land-Use Change, and Forestry*. Cambridge: Cambridge University Press. https://www.ipcc.ch/report/land-use-land-use-change-and-forestry/.

WTO (World Trade Organization). 2021. "Chair Summary Following COVID-19 and Vaccine Equity: What Can the WTO Contribute." Speech by D. G. Okonjo. WTO, Geneva. https://www.wto.org/english/news_e/spno_e/spno5_e.htm.

Wu, Zhiheng, Hou Guisheng, and Xin Baogui. 2020. "The Causality between Participation in GVCs, Renewable Energy Consumption, and CO_2 Emissions." *Sustainability 2020* 12 (3): 1237. https://doi.org/10.3390/su12031237.

Yara International ASA. 2021. "Fertilizer Life Cycle Perspective." Yara International ASA, Oslo. https://www.yara.com/crop-nutrition/why-fertilizer/environment/fertilizer-life-cycle/.

Zhan, James X., Bruno Casella, and Richard Bolwijn. 2020. "Towards a New Generation of Special Economic Zones: Sustainable and Competitive." In *Oxford Handbook on Industrial Hubs and Economic Development*, edited by Arkebe Oqubay and Justin Yifu Lin. Oxford: Oxford University Press.

3

Evolving Comparative Advantages and the Impacts of Extreme Weather Events

Low- and middle-income countries are especially vulnerable to climate change. Figure 3.1 presents an index of vulnerability—the University of Notre Dame Global Adaptation Initiative (ND-GAIN) Country Index (n.d.)[1]—showing that low-income and lower-middle-income countries are clustered at higher values of the index. This clustering occurs because agriculture is the main economic activity in most low-income countries, which therefore are highly vulnerable to the effects of climate change. Analysis across countries finds a significant increase in low- and middle-income countries' exposure to climate-induced changes of sea-level rise and storm surges (Dasgupta et al. 2011). These countries are also the least able to deal (financially) with the consequences of climate change and have the lowest capacity to adapt to it.

Trade is a key mechanism through which climate change will influence the economic outcomes of low- and middle-income countries. Rising temperatures and changing patterns of precipitation will affect the capacity of countries to produce goods and services to meet their export and import needs. More frequent extreme weather events will compromise capital investments in trade-related activities and alter the availability of labor through migration. At the same time, trade plays a critical role in recovering from weather-related crises and in adapting to the long-term implications of climate change.

This chapter briefly reviews how climate change will affect the comparative advantages of low- and middle-income countries, with a focus on agriculture. It finds that trade in agricultural products will become more important in satisfying global food needs as average temperatures rise and patterns of precipitation undergo significant changes. Climate change is also increasing the frequency and intensity of extreme weather events. Again, trade is vital for a country's recovery from such disasters, and a numerical simulation shows the huge repercussions that barriers to trade, such as export restrictions, can have for the economic costs of weather-related catastrophes.

FIGURE 3.1 ND-GAIN Index: Vulnerability to Climate Change in Selected Countries, by Income Level, 2019

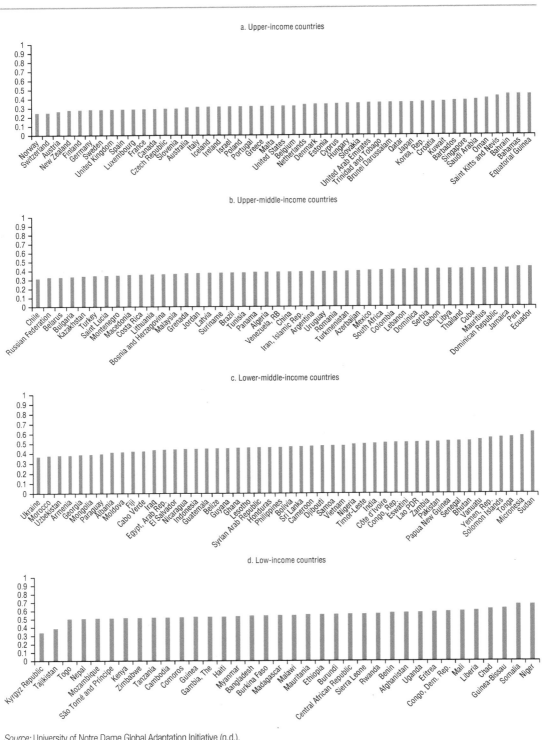

Source: University of Notre Dame Global Adaptation Initiative (n.d.).

While facing immense adaptation challenges, substantial new opportunities will arise for countries to diversify their exports in a global, low-carbon economy. The challenges relate to the unavoidable changes in long-standing comparative advantages, while new opportunities will arise from the application of new, low-carbon technologies that will allow countries to exploit their own carbon competitiveness. This phenomenon is already apparent for environmentally preferable products,[2] for example, but it will require lower tariffs and fewer regulatory barriers in importing countries and investments in the capacity to trade and verify carbon footprints.

The impact of a changing climate on comparative advantages

Climate change will manifest itself mainly in higher temperatures, pluvial and river floods, sea-level rise, melting ice caps, and other weather-related conditions—all having a direct impact on how and what kinds of goods and services are traded. These impacts will, in turn, have implications for the pattern of global investment and may lead to substantial changes in migration patterns.[3] The impacts on the agriculture sector are the most obvious. Regions currently producing and exporting a particular crop may lose their comparative advantage at higher temperatures, which are likely to result in lower yields, while other, currently colder regions may gain a comparative advantage in that crop. Additional, indirect effects may result, such as an increase in the prevalence of plant and animal pests as well as a rise in the incidence of diseases that lower yields. Unfortunately, while strategies for controlling and eliminating these pathogens may exist, trade restrictions may hamper their availability.

Climate change will also affect other export activities of importance, such as services that are offered primarily outside or through travel, especially tourism. Tourism is a key source of revenue and jobs in many low- and middle-income countries. The sector is both highly vulnerable to climate change and a major actor in exacerbating greenhouse gas emissions through, for example, its impact on demand for air travel. The tourism sector is especially vulnerable to climate change in Africa, the Middle East, South Asia, and the small island developing states, typically in countries where tourism accounts for the largest share of gross domestic product (GDP) and regions where tourism is expected to grow strongly. Hence, climate change will increasing undermine tourism's role in driving development and poverty reduction in these vulnerable countries (Scott, Hall, and Gössling 2019, among others).

Nonetheless, there are ways to facilitate the development of sustainable and resilient tourism. Gössling and Higham (2021) suggest that significant opportunities exist for low- and middle-income economies. Specifically, for hotels and accommodation businesses, it is always economically feasible to reduce energy use (20 percent at zero investment). Destinations could also develop optimization models focused on closer extended-length-of-stay, all-year tourism. They propose a high-value, low-carbon, resilient tourism "destination model for the future" that is centered on reducing leakage, lowering carbon, and adding value. Throughout the sector, a best practice would be for all tourism stakeholders to support and lobby for low-carbon policies, including carbon dioxide (CO_2) taxes ("environmental fees"). The public sector also has a key role to play, particularly to incentivize sustainability. For example, in Sri Lanka, new tourism investments should follow sustainable guidelines.

Since agricultural activities tend to be more sensitive to climate change than industrial activities, agricultural trade is likely to be affected the most. The vulnerability of agricultural yields to climate entails changes that threaten not only domestic food security but also the competitiveness and market share of food-exporting countries. These effects will, in turn, impinge significantly on their economic development and ability to eliminate poverty. Table 3.1 summarizes the mechanisms by which climate change will affect crop yields. Outcomes may not always be negative and will vary across and within countries. Most studies of climate change and its impacts on agriculture have focused on crop production—the area where modeling infrastructure has been developed most fully. However, agricultural productivity will also suffer from a drop in labor productivity attributable to rising temperatures. Indeed, in the tropics, the impact of heat stress may be greater on humans than on (adapted) crops. Hence, the estimated costs of climate change would probably be higher for low- and middle-income countries located in the tropics if the analysis were extended beyond the direct impacts of climate change on crop yields to include the indirect effect on labor productivity as well (Hertel and de Lima 2020).

TABLE 3.1 Factors Affected by Climate Change and Impact on Crop Productivity

Biophysical factor	Temperature	CO_2 concentration	Temperate vs. tropical impacts
Crop development	Faster development and shorter grain-filling stage reduce yields; yields are higher when water stress occurs at the end of the season than at the beginning	—	—
Photosynthesis and respiration	Warming can either increase or decrease net carbon uptake, depending on the type of crop, starting temperature, and day and nighttime warming; higher temperatures increase VPD, which can lead to water stress	Increased stomatal conductance raises water use efficiency; photosynthesis rates and optimum temperature are raised for C3 plants[a]	Tropical crops are already at or above optimal temperature, so increases are detrimental; lack of adequate nutrients constrains gains from increased CO_2; greater prevalence of tuber crops and dry conditions benefit tropical agriculture, but are offset by lower share of C3 crops
Water stress	Heightened VPD leads to higher soil evaporation and plant transpiration and lower soil moisture	Water use is more efficient	Lower soil moisture is more constraining in the tropics; the length of growing period could decline by 20% in Africa
Extreme temperature damage	Both cold and hot extremes can damage plant cells; extreme heat during flowering increases sterility	Sterility from exposure to high temperatures is exacerbated by elevated CO_2 caused by increased canopy warming	Higher temperatures benefit temperate crops by reducing frost constraints; tropical crops are more likely hit by extreme heat effects
Pests and disease damage	Invasive weeds are more climate tolerant and more responsive to changes in temperature because of their short juvenile period and long-distance dispersal; reduced frequency of frost expands the range of pests and diseases	Invasive weeds are more responsive to changes in elevated CO_2 concentrations caused by short juvenile period and long-distance dispersal; elevated CO_2 can make weed management more difficult	Increased extreme events reduce biotic resistance of native plants, providing openings for invasive species

Source: Hertel and Lobell 2014.

Note: CO_2 = carbon dioxide; VPD = vapor pressure deficit.

a. A "normal" plant—one that does not have photosynthetic adaptations to reduce photorespiration—is called a C3 plant. C3 plants include barley, oats, rice, and wheat as well as cotton, sunflowers, soybeans, sugar beets, potatoes, and tobacco.

Estimates of the impacts of climate change on crop yields by country and by region suggest that comparative advantages in agriculture will change significantly. While the precise impacts of climate change are marked by considerable uncertainties—and different models, which are built on varying specifications and parameter values, can produce different results—the available studies clearly show that climate change will alter comparative advantages in agriculture. Table 3.2 provides indicative estimates of changes in crop yields and suggests substantial differences in impacts across regions for a given crop and across crops globally. Again, while most projected impacts are negative, for certain crops in particular regions, climate change will boost yields. These regional estimates hide important impacts at the country level and within countries. Hence, not only do these expected changes in yield suggest that the current structure of trade will change significantly, but also that trade will be key to climate adaptation efforts—by adjusting the type (and volume) of crops grown in particular regions. In fact, adjustments to production and trade flows may play a large role in attenuating the impacts of climate change.

Estimates of the overall impacts of climate change on crop production at the country level are shown in table 3.3 for selected low- and middle-income countries. The importance of crop production in overall economic activity correlates with the impact of climate change on productivity, in this case an approximation of the impact on welfare. For most countries, the impact of climate change on productivity is important but not huge. For example, Indonesia is the median country in the study conducted by Costinot, Donaldson, and Smith (2016), where the estimated change in average productivity corresponds to a 1.26 percent decline in total GDP. However, some countries may see their crop productivity severely affected by climate change. The GDP of the Democratic Republic of Congo could drop by as much as 7 percent, while that of Malawi, the most vulnerable country in this sample, could drop by more than 38 percent.

A focused review of the literature highlights the risks involved for low- and middle-income countries. Barua and Valenzuela (2018) find that increases in

TABLE 3.2 Impact of Climate Change on Crop Yields, Accounting for CO_2 Fertilization, by Region

Region	Maize	Rice	Wheat	Other crops	All crops
Asia	15.3	3.9	−53.5	−12.8	−8.9
Commonwealth of Independent States	−9.7	n.a.	−1.5	−2.0	−2.3
Europe	−15.1	51.5	−8.2	−11.6	−11.1
Latin America	3.3	−36.9	−35.3	−38.9	−35.4
Middle East and North Africa	115.5	−87.2	−25.9	−29.1	−23.0
North America	−15.7	9.1	−5.1	−18.4	−16.2
Oceania	20.9	−32.4	−40.0	−16.7	−19.8
Sub-Saharan Africa	0.0	−15.3	−76.3	−42.6	−38.7
World	1.5	3.2	−33.3	−17.2	−13.2

Source: GAEZ (Global Agro-Ecological Zones) project of the Food and Agriculture Organization and the International Institute for Applied Systems Analysis, as presented by Gouel and Laborde 2018.
Note: Maize = corn. Gouel and Laborde 2018 simulate a counterfactual scenario of climate change where the shock on crop yields at the 2080 horizon is based on simulations from crop science. n.a. = not applicable.

TABLE 3.3 Estimated Changes in Aggregate Productivity due to the Impact of Climate Change on Crop Production in Selected Countries, at the 2080 Horizon

Country	Crop output as a % of GDP	Average change in productivity (%)
Bangladesh	12.4	−3.4
Brazil	3.2	−1.9
Cameroon	9.4	−3.1
Congo, Dem. Rep.	15.4	−7.0
Egypt, Arab Rep.	5.3	−2.0
Ethiopia	11.9	−3.8
Indonesia	8.1	−1.3
Malawi	74.9	−38.4
Thailand	6.1	−2.6
Uganda	33.8	−3.8

Source: Costinot, Donaldson, and Smith 2016.

temperature affect the agricultural exports of both high-income and low- and middle-income economies, but the impact is much larger for the latter. A percentage increase in temperature lowers the agricultural exports of low- and middle-income countries by almost 13 percent and those of high-income countries by less than 6 percent. Agricultural exports from lower-middle-income and lower-income countries are at an even greater risk from rising temperatures—a 1°C increase in temperature leads to a 23 percent fall in the agricultural exports of lower-middle-income countries and a drop of 39 percent in those of low-income countries. Higher levels of precipitation also have a negative impact on exports—the effect being significant for lower-middle-income and low-income economies.

International trade plays a critical role in global food security. The impact of climate change on comparative advantages and trade flows is therefore key to addressing food insecurity in low- and middle-income countries in the future. Estimates from the International Food Policy Research Institute (IFPRI) show how climate change will severely undermine progress on food security (figure 3.2). By 2030 it is predicted that an additional 70 million people will be at risk of hunger because of climate change. This increase will be concentrated in South Asia and Sub-Saharan Africa. Similarly, by 2050, the number of people at risk of hunger will be almost 20 percent higher by the same token. More than half of this predicted increase in hunger will occur in Sub-Saharan Africa. The challenge of climate change and food insecurity will be greatest in countries that typically already are food insecure. These countries include fragile and conflict-affected states, many of which are among the most vulnerable to a changing climate. These countries are likely to become even more dependent on food imports. Food insecurity is, in turn, associated with fragility, and higher food prices increase the risk of protests, rioting, and civil conflict.

FIGURE 3.2 Hunger with and without Climate Change in 2030 and 2050, by Region

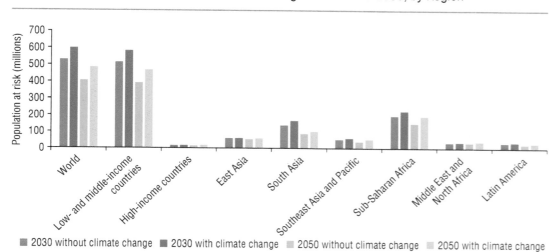

■ 2030 without climate change   ■ 2030 with climate change   ■ 2050 without climate change   ■ 2050 with climate change

Source: International Food Policy Research Institute.

These projections suggest that international trade will have to play an even greater role in addressing food security in a climate-affected world. International trade reduces food insecurity and malnutrition during periods of domestic shortages by increasing access to food and attenuating price volatility.[4] More generally, countries that are structurally food deficient rely on trade to satisfy domestic demand. Global production tends to be less volatile than production at the country level, so trade can play a risk-sharing role in the face of uncertainty over domestic production. Since climate change will increase the volatility of food production at the national level, trade will gain importance in reducing price volatility and delivering food supplies to countries (Smith and Glauber 2019).

Without expanded trade, more households in low-income countries will become food insecure as a result of climate change. IFPRI projections show that while climate change will account for lower trade in agricultural products in 2050, relative to the scenario of no climate change, trade in all of the main food products will be higher in absolute terms. Thus, trade will become increasingly important for food security. The issue is whether the policy environment for trade in agricultural products will be conducive to such an increase in trade or whether trade restrictions and uncertainty over their use could hamper investments in food production. Further, additional liberalization of trade in agricultural products could increase the contribution of trade to resolving food insecurity in a climate-constrained world.

As for tariffs, substantial protection of agriculture persists (table 3.4). Not captured in the table is that tariffs tend to increase with the degree of processing, offering extremely high levels of effective protection and inflated consumer prices for processed agricultural products. Hence, substantial opportunities exist to expand the global market for food products through tariff reductions.

There is considerable evidence that tariffs are not the main form of protection in the case of agricultural products. Nontariff barriers—including licensing requirements

TABLE 3.4 Average Most-Favored-Nation Unweighted Tariffs on Agricultural Products in Selected Countries and Regions, 2019

Country or region	Meat and offal	Dairy, eggs, and natural honey	Edible vegetables, roots, and tubers	Edible fruits and nuts	Cereals	WTO agricultural
Brazil	9.94	14.92	8.87	10.54	5.06	10.09
China	18.24	13.54	10.97	18	11.69	12.97
India	32.12	33.85	31.59	35.76	32.31	36.24
United States	4.22	12.66	8.59	3.43	1.53	7.03
EU27	5.18	5.34	8.67	6.88	1.44	6.09
East Asia and Pacific	7.01	6.85	6.36	7.02	2.9	6.23
Latin America and Caribbean	16.44	15.80	13.83	18.32	7.05	13.06
Middle East and North Africa	22.34	14.95	14.85	16.87	4.31	18.07
South Asia	21.52	24.04	20.74	24.22	17.89	22.39
Sub-Saharan Africa	21.84	18.89	17.22	17.15	8.42	14.49

Source: World Integrated Trade Solution.

Note: WTO = World Trade Organization. EU27 = 27 European Union member countries: Austria, Belgium, Bulgaria, Croatia, Cyprus, Czech Republic, Denmark, Estonia, Finland, France, Germany, Greece, Hungary, Ireland, Italy, Latvia, Lithuania, Luxembourg, Malta, the Netherlands, Poland, Portugal, Romania, Slovakia, Slovenia, Spain, and Sweden.

for both imports and exports; arbitrary sanitary and phytosanitary standards not based on scientific evidence; and customs and other import procedures that are slow, costly, and excessive—are major challenges for agricultural exporters in many regions. These barriers raise food prices, undermine food quality, affect food availability, and impose extra burdens on small businesses.

One of the biggest risks for food security in food-importing countries during times of crisis is the imposition of export restrictions by exporting countries. In previous global crises such as the financial crisis of 2008/09, producing nations resorted to limits on food exports that hurt consumers around the world. Without some form of international agreement, this issue will occur again in future crises and will likely become more critical, given the way in which climate change affects patterns of production and trade. Limits on export quantities are set despite the clear consensus among economists that export restrictions and precautionary purchases of food by a small number of key countries can lead to a rapid rise in global prices and severe shortages in other countries. Hence, some form of coordination and discipline is needed when such policies are adopted.

Economic theory and substantial empirical analysis over a long period of experience with export restraints show that export restrictions by large producers increase the volatility of supply and prices. Export restraints by large agricultural producers limit overall supply in the global economy, which reduces the availability of products in countries that need them the most: low-income countries with substantial levels of poverty and limited or no capacity to increase their own production.[5] While, in the short run, limits on exports may result in lower domestic prices and a higher domestic supply of food products in the countries imposing those measures, they reduce the incentives to invest in food production and can reduce supply in the long run, not only at the global level but also in those export-restricting countries. These types of measures may provoke retaliatory measures that further disrupt global markets and possibly make it even harder for poor countries to procure essential supplies.

The following measures can help to protect low-income countries from export restrictions that limit access to critical food and other essential products in food production, such as seeds and fertilizers:

• *Increase information and transparency and monitoring.* Decisions on export restrictions are influenced by perceived risks and the fear of domestic shortages. Moreover, politically well-connected domestic actors who benefit from export restrictions, such as food processors, may also seek to affect such decisions. Policy makers require data and information that allow them to assess these risks accurately and the capacity to mitigate them, both domestically and through coordination with other countries. Improved information on global markets and greater transparency and information sharing can help to limit panic-driven policy decisions and contribute to more informed and coordinated responses that avoid price surges. Information on global food stocks, for example, is crucial for policy makers trying to assess the risk of impending food shortages. Indeed, the lack of reliable data on stocks of grains and oilseeds and deficiencies in the monitoring of food prices undoubtedly exacerbated the export restrictions that destabilized global food markets during the global financial crisis of 2007/08. Subsequent investments by the G-20 countries in food information systems have improved the quality of information available to policy makers and may have tempered the use of export restrictions on food during the COVID-19 (coronavirus) pandemic.[6] Transparency and information sharing will become even more important as climate change induces greater variability in production and heightened uncertainty.

• *Increase cooperation on trade issues that are critical for health and food security.* The risk that producing countries might impose export restrictions may be sufficient to dissuade importing countries from fully liberalizing tariffs. In fact, the use of export restrictions by a small number of countries has fomented the view that other countries should increase their tariff protection and enhance support for domestic production through other means. This approach limits the overall global market for food, lowering investment and employment in farms in the large producing countries and increasing volatility at the global level. Ideally, it would form the basis for an agreement among producing countries to ban the use of export restrictions in return for tariff liberalization by importing countries. Such an agreement would reduce policy uncertainty and the risks associated with global markets in essential products.

Some economies have taken steps within existing regional agreements to deepen cooperation on trade in essential products. New Zealand and Singapore have committed to remove customs duties and refrain from imposing export restrictions on 124 essential goods, including food and health care products.[7] In early 2020, a group of 22 World Trade Organization (WTO) members committed not to restrict agricultural exports and agreed that emergency measures related to agriculture and agricultural food products designed to tackle COVID-19 must be targeted, proportionate, transparent, and temporary.[8] These initiatives provide a base from which to move to multilateral coordination at the WTO—aimed at providing effective discipline on agricultural export restrictions to allow for greater certainty of agricultural trade in a climate-affected world.

Extreme weather events and trade

Climate change is leading to more frequent and severe extreme weather events. According to the United Nations, climate-related disasters increased by 83 percent in the first two decades of the 21st century compared to the last two decades of the 20th century—from 3,656 to 6,681 events. Major floods have more than doubled; the number of severe storms has increased by 40 percent; and droughts, wildfires, and heat waves have become much more prevalent.

Extreme weather-related shocks such as storms, floods, and droughts have wide-ranging implications for trade at the macro level and for sectors, products, and firms. Exports from, and imports to, the affected area will be directly affected during the crisis and in the aftermath if trade-related transport and logistics infrastructure has sustained significant damage. Longer-term adverse impacts on exports will result from loss of life and injury of employees as well as damage to the capital stock (buildings, machinery) and inventories of exporting firms. These effects will be compounded if exporting firms are unable to continue exporting because of the damage or the cancellation of contracts following inability to fulfill orders during the crisis and its aftermath. Countries exporting agricultural products will suffer severe damages if an extreme weather shock affects the planting or harvesting of their main crops. Imports are critical to immediate recovery from a natural disaster. Trade allows the crisis-induced shortage of supply in critical goods and services (food, medicines, emergency workers) to be met by imports from unaffected countries. During the reconstruction, imports provide access to the equipment, materials, and skills that are necessary to rebuild the capital stock and transport infrastructure.

Although the immediate impacts of a climate disaster on economic activity are most apparent, the long-term impacts, particularly on development in low-income countries, can be enormous. Given their limited resources and capacities, poorer countries tend to recover more slowly and more partially than richer countries—especially when the fiscal space limits the funds available for reconstruction. This situation is aggravated by the increasing likelihood of recurrent natural disasters disrupting the same economies, which will have profound long-term implications for population and migration, investment, and trade in those locations. The immediate impact of a natural disaster on trade often is a sharp decline in the trade balance as imports of food, raw materials, and reconstruction materials rise while exports fall. This deteriorating trade balance has longer-term implications for macroeconomic management.

Yet short-term impacts can also have adverse long-term development outcomes. For example, if malnutrition increases during the crisis and children become stunted or if schools are closed for a significant period, a country's long-term development will be jeopardized. When a cyclone, flood, or drought hits Mozambique, per capita food consumption drops by up to 30 percent—about 0.4 fewer meals per person per day. In Zambia, the drought that accompanied the 2015/16 El Niño season lowered affected households' maize (corn) yields by about 20 percent and their income by up to 37 percent. More generally, the adverse impacts of natural disasters tend to affect specific groups of society disproportionately: the poor and marginalized; women; and micro, small, and medium enterprises, which are much less able to bear the costs than larger firms.

Trade can spread the impact of localized weather shocks such as floods beyond the area specifically affected but also can support resilience and recovery. The overall impact will tend to be context specific, but in general the more sophisticated the global value chain and the more specialized the inputs being traded, the fewer substitution possibilities there are likely to be and the greater the transmission of the shock. Major floods in Thailand in 2011, for example, had substantial impacts on downstream firms in sectors such as automobiles and computers in other countries. Hence, the trade of low- and middle-income countries may be affected by extreme weather events elsewhere in the world—in countries that supply key inputs for trade activities or where buyers are located. Trade, particularly supply-chain links through regional and global value chains, have a role in propagating the initial shock over a wider area, making low- and middle-income countries more vulnerable in this context.

Trade and global value chains may amplify shocks across countries through various mechanisms, but other processes promote resilience during a crisis. In general, trade tends to benefit the firms and people directly affected by an extreme weather event but can also have an (indirect) impact on firms and people outside the area hit. In the United States, exposure to the shock of the Japanese earthquake in 2011 had a more substantial impact on the affiliates of Japanese multinationals than on non-Japanese firms. The affiliates of Japanese firms in the United States were unable to find substitute inputs in the short run (Boehm, Flaaen, and Pandalai-Nayar 2019). The degree of substitutability between inputs from different locations is therefore an important factor in determining the transmission of weather-related shocks to firms. By contrast, following Hurricane Sandy in the United States, some negative impacts on damaged firms were propagated to upstream and downstream suppliers and customers within the United States but not to overseas firms. The negative impact on the suppliers and customers of damaged firms appears to have been significantly lower if the firms were also connected to foreign firms and were relatively large (in terms of number of workers). Large firms and firms linked to global value chains have greater opportunities to substitute away from suppliers and customers negatively affected by economic shocks because they face lower search costs relative to sales than smaller firms and firms without international connections. Certain characteristics of global value chains are conducive to greater resilience following a shock. The costs of establishing supplier networks can encourage lead firms to maintain relationships with suppliers during a crisis rather than terminate them. As in the case of the COVID-19 pandemic, lead firms sometimes provide financial and technical support to suppliers during a crisis.

The structure of a network matters in determining the extent of propagation of shocks—based on the presence of influential nodes, the degree of clustering, and the extent of substitutability between nodes. Studies based on information from detailed firm-level surveys on the connections between firms (in the role of customers and suppliers) and the customers of customers and suppliers of suppliers support these conclusion (Kashiwagi, Matous, and Todo 2018). A network's key characteristics tend to vary with different types of products, and initial empirical evidence suggests that they are particularly relevant for parts and components of machinery, such as vehicles and electronics.

An interesting implication of the contagion of shocks within supply chains is that the beneficial effects of government support to enhance the resilience of supply chains can be magnified beyond the direct recipients to other firms in the value chain (Kashiwagi and Todo 2020). For example, after the earthquake in Japan, subsidies that were provided to small and medium enterprises to support the repair and reinstallation of damaged capital goods and facilities indirectly benefited other firms in disaster-affected areas linked through supply chains that did not receive any subsidy. It would be interesting to establish whether, in cases where global value chains link firms across countries, government interventions targeting national firms also have had some benefit for linked firms in other countries.

However, very few studies have looked explicitly at the impact of extreme weather shocks and adjustments within global value chains on firms in, and the trade of, low- and middle-income countries. Initial evidence on the impact of the COVID-19 crisis suggests that the trade flows of poorer countries are more likely to cease than those of richer countries.[9] If firms in low- and middle-income countries face higher costs to find substitute suppliers or buyers, they will probably be affected more severely by extreme weather events that compromise existing sources of raw materials or intermediate inputs or major markets for their product. In addition, impacts on small low- and middle-income countries, especially island economies, will tend to be augmented by the limited trade-related transport and logistics. Many low- and middle-income countries are dependent on a single port of entry or a single trade corridor, which can be severely disrupted by severe weather and alternative routes or ports are not available.

Disaster response and trade restrictions: Implications from a numerical model

As the pandemic and global warming continue, there is a growing probability that COVID-19 surges and extreme weather events, such as flooding, will collide (Phillips et al. 2020). Assessing the risks of a pandemic and extreme weather events separately may mask significant vulnerabilities that appear only in a multihazard framework. Such a perspective is likely to be particularly useful from a global trade perspective since the global trade network will be particularly important when countries are affected by major shocks from which they cannot recover without help. With limited discipline on trade restrictions, such as barriers to exports, there is the added risk that trade policy decisions will deepen the adverse impact of these compound events and slow the recovery. Measures to combat one crisis may jeopardize measures to combat another one and ultimately exacerbate the negative impacts of both. The interaction between pandemic control and flood responses is different than that between two flood events. Flood events are usually sudden or rapid-onset events that require immediate emergency measures, while pandemics last longer, and the corresponding control measures of various durations could coincide with different flood periods. These differences in responses between pandemics and multiflood situations increase the complexity of economic impact assessment. An approach is required that considers not only the parallel threats of individual hazards on population and physical assets but also the side effects of virus containment on postflood recovery and the role of trade in disaster recovery (box 3.1).

BOX 3.1 Numerical Model to Explore the Economic Impacts of Compound Hazards and Trade Restrictions

The impact model stems from the adaptive regional input-output (ARIO) model, which is widely used in the realm of single-hazard analysis to simulate the propagation of negative shocks throughout the economy (Hallegatte 2014; Hallegatte and Ghil 2008). Compared with traditional input-output (IO) and computable general equilibrium (CGE) models, the ARIO model is an agent-based model that offers the simplicity of IO modeling and has the flexibility of CGE modeling. This model is extended to allow for cross-regional substitutability of suppliers, to be able to assess the global supply-chain effects of COVID-19 control measures and flood responses. The model analyzes the interaction between climate and pandemic responses—that is, the negative externality of pandemic control for the recovery of capital destroyed by natural disasters and the stimulus effects of capital reconstruction to offset the negative impacts of pandemic control. Second, it considers the role of export restrictions and production specialization in exacerbating the economic consequences of the compound events. It does so by varying the substitutability of regional products to investigate the effect of production specialization in different sectors.

This compound-hazard impact model is applied to a hypothetical global economy that consists of four regions and five sectors. The four regions—regions A, B, C, and D—account for 21 percent, 39 percent, 28 percent, and 12 percent of the global economy, respectively. Region C is the only region that is hit by flooding amid a global pandemic. Region B is the largest trading partner of region C. More than half (52 percent) of C's total trading volume—equivalent to 11 percent of C's output—comes from region B. Next in line are regions A and D, accounting for 31 percent and 17 percent of C's total trading volume, respectively. The five sectors are agriculture, general manufacturing, capital manufacturing, construction, and other services. Capital manufacturing and construction are the two sectors involved in reconstructing capital damaged by flooding. It is assumed that capital reconstruction relies largely on local inputs of capital goods and construction services. For example, the construction and capital manufacturing sectors of region C account for 68 percent and 20 percent of the reconstruction in region C, respectively, while the capital manufacturing and construction sectors of region B and the capital manufacturing sector of region A account for the remaining 12 percent of construction. The model is run on a weekly basis in this study.

Three scenarios of flooding are explored: a *small flood*, affecting 20 percent of the population in region C; a *medium flood*, affecting 40 percent of its population; and a *large flood*, affecting 60 percent. At the same time as the flooding occurs, regions affected by the pandemic take measures to bring its spread under control. The strictness of the control policy, which is measured by the percentage reduction in transportation capacity due to lockdown measures relative to the predisaster level, is benchmarked at 30 percent for 24 weeks. The direct economic impacts of the collision of these disasters arise from (1) the shortage or malfunction of production factors (productive capital and labor), reducing firms' production capacity; (2) the impact on infrastructure, specifically on transportation critical to linking the supplies and demands of different agents in the economic networks, because transportation failures increase the inaccessibility to production materials and interrupt production activities; and (3) the impact on final demands, leading to structural, short-term changes in the overall mix during or after the event. Export restrictions are included progressively in the form of a 25 percent, 50 percent, and 75 percent reduction in export volume.

For more details on the model and the scenarios, see and AghaKouchak et al. (2020) and Hu et al. (2021).

Two major conclusions can be drawn from the simulation results. The first conclusion concerns the economic interplay between pandemic control and flood responses. On the one hand, the concurrence of pandemic control during a flood event hampers the postflood recovery and engenders extra economic losses. This effect confirms the idea that, from an economic perspective, restrictions targeted at COVID-19 containment result in inadequate responses to flooding, aggravating the flood impacts (Ishiwatari et al. 2020; Selby and Kagawa 2020; Srivastava 2020). On the other hand, a flood disaster exacerbates the pandemic impacts only when the flood damage is large enough to exceed the stimulus effect from the flood-related reconstruction activities. Such a stimulus effect could alleviate some of the negative impacts of pandemic control if the scale of flooding is not large. Further, when pandemic control measures are taken after flooding, the economic impacts are more severe than when they are implemented before flooding, because of the longer-lasting disruption of the postflood recovery.

The second conclusion refers to the role of trade in the economic footprint of the compound risks. When increasing trade barriers intertwine with the collision of flooding and pandemic control, a triangled "perfect storm" is created. Export restrictions increase global economic losses, and the increments of the losses increase with the degree of the export restriction. While all regions suffer from export restrictions, those that depend more heavily on regional trade are more vulnerable to a universal export restriction. Specialization that leads to the concentration of production of key sectors in particular regions and limits substitution possibilities raises the vulnerability of the economic network to such compound risks. Finally, export restrictions imposed on specialized sectors can trigger devastating impacts on the global economy at a time when it is already dealing with the compound hazards of extreme weather and a pandemic.

Table 3.5 presents the global indirect impacts of a "perfect storm," relative to predisaster levels, under different export restriction scenarios. Compared to the free-trade scenario, a 25 percent export restriction increases global economic losses by

TABLE 3.5 Indirect Impacts on Global GDP of a "Perfect Storm" under Different Export Restriction Scenarios
Percentage impact

	Pandemic control		
Scenario	Small flood	Medium flood	Large flood
Free trade	−12.43	−12.64	−13.71
Export restriction			
25%	−14.23	−14.36	−15.65
50%	−16.41	−16.43	−17.77
75%	−19.03	−19.06	−20.16

Sources: World Bank data; Hu et al. 2021.
Note: Impacts are measured with respect to the predisaster levels of annual global GDP.

1.81 percent, 1.72 percent, and 1.94 percent, respectively, when a small, medium, or large flood intersects with global pandemic control; a 50 percent export restriction adds another 2.18 percent, 2.07 percent, and 2.12 percent to global losses, respectively, compared to the 25 percent export restriction; and finally, a 75 percent export restriction adds another 2.62 percent, 2.63 percent, and 2.39 percent to global losses, compared to the 50 percent export restriction. Thus, stronger export restrictions result in larger economic losses.

Regions that trade more intensively are more vulnerable to export restrictions than other regions. Figure 3.3 shows that the cumulative losses in region A grow by 2.90 percent, 6.25 percent, and 9.71 percent, when the export restriction increases from 0 percent to 25 percent, 50 percent, and 75 percent, respectively, during the confluence of a large flood and pandemic control. By comparison, region B is the least sensitive to the export restriction but still suffers considerable extra losses. This result may be related, in part, to the different degrees of trade dependence of the regional economies. Specifically, for regions A and D, their volumes of trade with other regions account for about 30 percent and 31 percent of their total output, respectively, which are higher than those of the other two regions (23 percent for B and 20 percent for C). Higher dependence on interregional trade increases economic vulnerability when countries impose trade restrictions.

Increased specialization and concentration of trade activities limit the degree of substitutability across regions and reduce countries' economic resilience against the compound flood and pandemic hazard. These results are illustrated in table 3.6 and figure 3.4, respectively. The greater extent of specialization involving some key node sectors (that is, the capital manufacturing sector in region B and the general manufacturing sector in region C in this case) increases the vulnerability of the global and regional economy to climate and pandemic disasters. When the substitution possibilities away from the capital manufacturing sector of region B and the general manufacturing sector of region C are limited as a result of specialization, the global economic losses rise by 0.02 percent (small flood), 0.14 percent (medium flood), and 0.92 percent (large flood), respectively, compared to the baseline scenario. Among the four regions, region B experiences the largest increase in gross value added (GVA) losses, followed by regions A and D, while region C has the smallest increase. For example, during the compound crises with a large flood, specialization of the three sectors saddles region B with extra losses of 1.31 percent, more than that of region A (1.21 percent), D (1.11 percent), and C (0.08 percent). Reduced substitutability of important intermediate products as a result of specialization makes firms in regions B, A, and D suffer earlier and longer-lasting shortages of inventories (that is, a sudden drop in their GVA) and therefore higher economic losses than in the baseline scenario.

Finally, the impacts are devastating if export restrictions are imposed when there is specialized production. When a 50 percent export restriction is imposed on the three specialized sectors, the relative losses of global GDP reach as high as 28.84 percent (small flood), 29.31 percent (medium flood), and 30.72 percent (large flood), respectively, more than double the impacts under the baseline scenario (12.43 percent, 12.64 percent, and 13.71 percent, respectively). Under this scenario, all regions, including region C, see significant increases in their GVA losses. For example, the

FIGURE 3.3 Weekly Changes in Regional Gross Value Added Relative to Predisaster Levels, When Multiscale Floods Collide with Pandemic Control and Export Restrictions

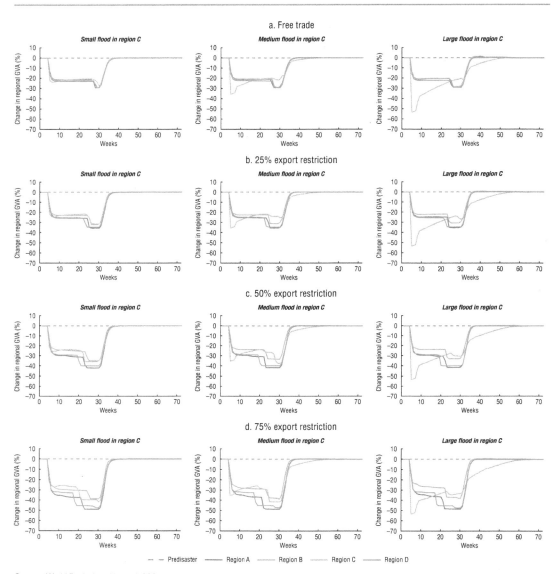

Sources: World Bank data; Hu et al. 2021.

Note: GVA = gross value added. The numbers in each plot indicate the cumulative losses or gains in regional GVAs over time, relative to the predisaster levels of the annual regional GVAs. Restrictions refer to exports of all goods and services from all regions.

relative GVA losses of region C increase by 13.88 percent because of the export restriction on specialized products, compared with the baseline scenario, when pandemic control and large flooding coincide.

The results from this highly stylized model show how important trade is to disaster recovery and that restrictions on exports during a crisis amplify the adverse economic impacts. This effect is attenuated in a world where specialization through trade and concentration of production in a few locations limit the opportunities for substituting suppliers. Policies that lead to higher trade barriers undermine the efforts of other countries simultaneously battling extreme weather events and a pandemic. The use of trade restrictions has a particularly detrimental impact on an integrated world economy that is marked by production specialization in key sectors. This finding confirms the need for effective discipline at the regional and global levels on the use of such measures in an increasingly integrated global economy.

TABLE 3.6 Indirect Impacts on Global GDP of a "Perfect Storm" under Different Production Specialization and Export Restriction Scenarios, Relative to Predisaster Levels
Percentage change

	Pandemic control		
Scenario	Small flood	Medium flood	Large flood
No specialization and export restriction	−12.43	−12.64	−13.71
Specialization in agriculture in region D	−12.42	−12.64	−13.72
Specialization in agriculture in region D, capital manufacturing in region B, and general manufacturing in region C	−12.44	−12.78	−14.63
Specialization in agriculture in region D, capital manufacturing in region B, and general manufacturing in region C with 50% export restriction	−28.84	−29.31	−30.72

Sources: World Bank data; Hu et al. 2021.

FIGURE 3.4 Weekly Changes in Regional GVA, Relative to Predisaster Levels, When Multiscale Floods Collide with Pandemic Control and Production Specialization

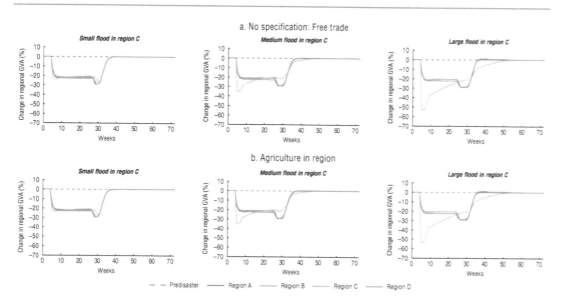

(Figure continues next page)

FIGURE 3.4 Weekly Changes in Regional GVA, Relative to Predisaster Levels, When Multiscale Floods Collide with Pandemic Control and Production Specialization *(Continued)*

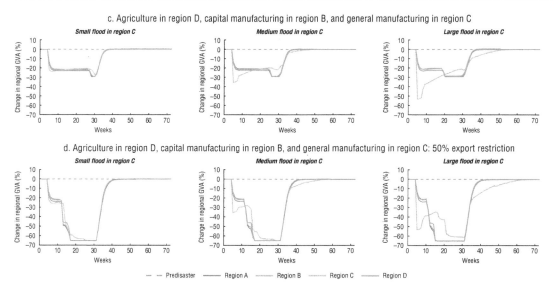

Sources: World Bank data; Hu et al. 2021.
Note: GVA = gross value added. The numbers in each plot indicate the cumulative loss or gain in regional GVA over time, relative to the predisaster levels of the annual regional GVA. From left to right, each column represents small-, medium-, and large-scale flooding in region C. From top to bottom, each row stands for one of the three specialization scenarios: (a) specialization only happens in the agriculture sector of region D; (b) specialization occurs in the agricultural sector of region D, the capital manufacturing sector of region B, and the general manufacturing sector of region C; or (c) specialization occurs in all three sectors, and all are hit with a 50 percent export restriction.

Conclusions

Climate change is having profound impacts on production and trade, especially in agriculture, and these impacts will get even worse in the coming decades. Given the importance of agriculture and the continuing challenge of food security, the impacts will be felt most strongly in low- and middle-income countries, particularly poor ones. For some low-income countries, the impacts could be catastrophic—that is, they could entail substantial reductions in income. Overall, the number of food-insecure people in low- and middle-income countries will increase substantially because of climate change. These countries are also the least prepared to adapt to climate change.

In an increasingly climate change–afflicted world, trade will gain importance as a mechanism to address food insecurity, support adaptation, and enable recovery from extreme weather events. Therefore, a trend toward deglobalization would compromise the ability of low- and middle-income countries to grow and reduce poverty as average global temperatures rise. In fact, opportunities exist to reduce barriers to trade in key products that will be affected by climate change and to facilitate countries' adjustment to changing comparative advantages and ability to respond effectively to climate-related disasters. These opportunities include the following:

- *Reducing tariff and nontariff barriers in low- and middle-income countries on key agricultural inputs for current technologies,* such as fertilizers, making it easier for farmers to improve their yields in the face of more adverse climate conditions

- *Facilitating access to new technologies for farmers in low- and middle-income countries through expedited seed release procedures and easier movement of agricultural specialists* who can share their knowledge on appropriate farming techniques in a climate-constrained world

- *Renewing efforts to reduce barriers to agricultural trade* (tariffs, nontariff barriers, domestic support, export restrictions), in both high-income and low- and middle-income countries, to increase (1) the size and stability of the global market for food products and (2) the opportunities for farmers in low- and middle-income countries to adapt to climate change and transition to new, more climate-resilient crops and products

- *Enhancing discipline at the global level on the use of measures such as export restrictions.* The increasing importance of trade, especially in agricultural products, entails greater risks for countries if access to imports of food is curtailed. Thus, a global deal seems within reach—one in which importing countries commit to reducing tariffs and other barriers (to expand the export market for producing firms), while exporting countries commit to using export control measures sparingly.

Opening up to trade entails adjustment costs for countries facing greater competition and needing to capture new, trade-related opportunities. These opportunities have typically received, at best, limited attention from policy makers. Perhaps with a focus on agriculture, an opportunity arises to take a broader approach and address the combined adjustments to trade and climate change.

Notes

1. The ND-GAIN Country Index summarizes a country's vulnerability to climate change and other global challenges in combination with its readiness to improve resilience.

2. Environmentally preferrable products are discussed in more detail in chapter 4 of this report.

3. The World Bank's flagship report on climate migration finds that—in Latin America, South Asia, and Sub-Saharan Africa—climate change will push millions of people to migrate within their own country by 2050 (Rigaud et al. 2018).

4. Trade is deemed a more efficient mechanism for stabilizing prices than domestic holdings of food stocks.

5. Models of global food demand and supply reinforce these conclusions. Export restrictions and precautionary purchases by a few large producing countries create rapid increases in global food prices and severe local food shortages. For example, if three major grain-exporting countries imposed full export bans, the price of wheat could rise by as much as 70 percent, while maize and rice prices could rise by 40 percent and 60 percent, respectively (Falkendal et al. 2021).

6. The Agricultural Market Information System (AMIS) was created in 2011; under it, (a) G-20 governments would instruct their statistical and other relevant agencies to provide timely and accurate data on food production, consumption, and stocks and to invest in necessary mechanisms and institutions if they did not exist; (b) international organizations would enhance global food security by monitoring, reporting, and analyzing market conditions and policies and by introducing a global early warning system; (c) a rapid response forum would promote policy coherence and coordination during crisis periods; and

(d) international organizations would support the improvement of national or regional monitoring systems in vulnerable low- and middle-income countries and regions. See AMIS Secretariat (2011).

7. For details, see the "Declaration on Trade in Essential Goods for Combating the Covid-19 Pandemic," April 15, 2020, https://www.beehive.govt.nz/sites/default/files/2020-04 /FINAL%20TEXT%20Declaration%20on%20Trade%20in%20 Essential%20Goods.pdf.

8. These members were the European Union; the United States; Australia; Brazil; Canada; Chile; Colombia; Costa Rica; Hong Kong SAR, China; Japan; Republic of Korea; Malawi; Mexico; New Zealand; Paraguay; Peru; Qatar; Singapore; Switzerland; Taiwan, China; Ukraine; and Uruguay.

9. For example, the COVID-19 pandemic disrupted global value chains, such as those involving apparel, with major clothing brands and retailers based in the European Union and United States canceling or postponing orders, including orders for goods already produced by suppliers in low- and middle-income countries and awaiting transportation. As a result, exporting firms in countries such as Bangladesh have gone out of business and workers have been laid off.

References

AghaKouchak, Amir, Felicia Chiang, Laurie S. Huning, Charlotte A. Love, Iman Mallakpour, Omar Mazdiyasni, Hamed Moftakhari, et al. 2020. "Climate Extremes and Compound Hazards in a Warming World." *Annual Review of Earth and Planetary Sciences* 48 (1): 519–48. https://doi.org/10.1146/annurev-earth-071719-055228.

AMIS (Agricultural Market Information System) Secretariat. 2011. "Enhancing Market Transparency." AMIS Secretariat, Rome. http://www.amis-outlook.org/fileadmin/user _upload/amis/docs/reports/Improving_global_governance_for_food_security.pdf.

Barua, Suborna, and Ernesto Valenzuela. 2018. "Climate Change Impacts on Global Agricultural Trade Patterns: Evidence from the Past 50 Years." Proceedings of the "Sixth International Conference on Sustainable Development 2018," Columbia University, New York, September 26–28. https://ssrn.com/abstract=3281550.

Boehm, Christoph E., Aaron Flaaen, and Nitya Pandalai-Nayar. 2019. "Input Linkages and the Transmission of Shocks: Firm-Level Evidence from the 2011 Tōhoku Earthquake." *Review of Economics and Statistics* 101 (1): 60–75.

Costinot, Arnaud, Dave Donaldson, and Cory Smith. 2016. "Evolving Comparative Advantage and the Impact of Climate Change in Agricultural Markets: Evidence from 1.7 Million Fields around the World." *Journal of Political Economy* 124 (1): 205–48. https://doi.org /10.1086/684719. https://www.mitpressjournals.org/doi/abs/10.1162/rest_a_00750.

Dasgupta, Susmita, Benoit Laplante, Siobhan Murray, and David Wheeler. 2011. "Exposure of Developing Countries to Sea-Level Rise and Storm Surges." *Climatic Change* 106 (4): 567–79.

Falkendal, Theresa, Christian Otto, Jacob Schewe, Jonas Jägermeyr, Megan Konar, Matti Kummu, Ben Watkins, and Michael J. Puma. 2021. "Grain Export Restrictions during COVID-19 Risk Food Insecurity in Many Low- and Middle-Income Countries." *Nature Food* 2: 11–14.

Gössling, Stefan, and James Higham. 2021 "The Low-Carbon Imperative: Destination Management under Urgent Climate Change." *Journal of Travel Research* 60 (6): 1167–79. https://doi.org/10.1177/0047287520933679.

Gouel, Christophe, and David Laborde. 2018. "The Crucial Role of International Trade in Adaptation to Climate Change." NBER Working Paper 25221, National Bureau of Economic Research, Cambridge, MA.

Hallegatte, Stéphane. 2014. *Natural Disasters and Climate Change: An Economic Perspective.* Cham: Springer. 10.1007/978-3-319-08933-1.

Hallegatte, Stéphane, and Michael Ghil. 2008. "Natural Disasters Impacting a Macroeconomic Model with Endogenous Dynamics." *Ecological Economics* 68 (1–2): 582–92. https://EconPapers.repec.org/RePEc:eee:ecolec:v:68:y:2008:i:1-2:p:582-592.

Hertel, Thomas W., and Cicero Z. de Lima. 2020. "Viewpoint: Climate Impacts on Agriculture: Searching for Keys under the Streetlight." *Food Policy* 95 (August): 101954.

Hertel, Thomas W., and David B. Lobell. 2014. "Agricultural Adaptation to Climate Change in Rich and Poor Countries: Current Modeling Practice and Potential for Empirical Contributions." *Energy Economics* 46 (C): 562–75. https://doi.org/10.1016/j.eneco.2014.04.014.

Hu, Yixin, Daoping Wang, Jingwen Huo, Lili Yang, Dabo Guan, Paul Brenton, and Vicky Chemutai. 2021. "Assessing the Economic Impacts of a 'Perfect Storm' of Extreme Weather, Pandemic Control and Deglobalization: A Methodological Construct." Working Paper, World Bank, Washington, DC. http://documents.worldbank.org/curated/en/744851623848784106/Assessing-the-Economic-Impacts-of-a-Perfect-Storm-of-Extreme-Weather-Pandemic-Control-and-Deglobalization-A-Methodological-Construct.

Ishiwatari, Mikio, Toshio Koike, Kenzo Hiroki, Takao Toda, and Tsukasa Katsube. 2020. "Managing Disasters amid COVID-19 Pandemic: Approaches of Response to Flood Disasters." *Progress in Disaster Science* 6 (April): 100096. https://doi.org/10.1016/j.pdisas.2020.100096.

Kashiwagi, Yuzuka, Petr Matous, and Yasuyuki Todo. 2018. "International Propagation of Economic Shocks through Global Supply Chains." WINPEC Working Paper E1810, Waseda Institute of Political Economy, Waseda University, Tokyo. https://www.waseda.jp/fpse/winpec/assets/uploads/2018/11/No.E1810.pdf.

Kashiwagi, Yuzuka, and Yasuyuki Todo. 2020. "The Propagation of the Economic Impact through Supply Chains: The Case of a Mega-City Lockdown to Contain the Spread of COVID-19." *PLoS One* 15 (9): e0239251. https://doi.org/10.1371/journal.pone.0239251.

Phillips, Carly, Astrid Caldas, Rachel Cleetus, Kristina A. Dahl, Juan Declet-Barreto, Rachel Licker, L. Delta Merner, et al. 2020. "Compound Climate Risks in the COVID-19 Pandemic." *Nature Climate Change* 10 (May 15): 586–88. https://doi.org/10.1038/s41558-020-0804-2.

Rigaud, Kanta Kumari, Alex de Sherbinin, Bryan Jones, Jonas Bergmann, Viviane Clement, Kayly Ober, Jacob Schewe, et al. 2018. *Groundswell: Preparing for Internal Climate Migration.* Washington, DC: World Bank. https://openknowledge.worldbank.org/handle/10986/29461.

Scott, Daniel, C. Michael Hall, and Stefan Gössling. 2019. "Global Tourism Vulnerability to Climate Change." *Annals of Tourism Research* 77 (July): 49–61.

Selby, David, and Fumiyo Kagawa. 2020. "Climate Change and Coronavirus: A Confluence of Two Emergencies as Learning and Teaching Challenge." *Policy and Practice: A Development Education Review* 30 (Spring): 104–14. https://www.developmenteducationreview.com/issue/issue-30/climate-change-and-coronavirus-confluence-two-emergencies-learning-and-teaching.

Smith, Vincent H., and Joseph W. Glauber. 2019. "The Future of U.S. Farm Policy." *Euro Choices,* April 21. https://doi.org/10.1111/1746-692X.12223.

Srivastava, Sanjay. 2020. "Disaster Risk Reduction and COVID-19 Pandemic: Changing Policy Perspective." Presentation at the 10th annual UN-SPIDER conference, "Lessons Learned during the Unprecedented Pandemic Situation," United Nations Office for Outer Space Affairs, Beijing, November 24–25.

University of Notre Dame Global Adaptation Initiative. No date. "Vulnerability: Country Rankings." https://gain-new.crc.nd.edu/ranking/vulnerability.

4

Adaptation to Climate Change: Trade in Green Goods and Services and Access to Low-Carbon Technologies

The implications for trade of adapting to a changing climate

Adaptation to climate change is already happening and can take place through the use of current technologies. For example, as temperatures rise, farmers can offset increasing nutrient constraints by applying additional fertilizer, combat the prevalence of weeds by using more machinery and labor, or offset lower yields by using irrigation. These adaptation techniques are especially challenging for low-income countries, which are the most vulnerable to climate change. Trade will play a key role in this adaptation process. For instance, crop selection and trade adjustments can help to mitigate the impacts of climate change. One study finds that changes in crops and trade adjustments reduce global losses from climate change by 55 percent and 43 percent, respectively (Gouel and Laborde 2018). Thus, how farmers respond to these challenges and opportunities will make a big difference to the overall impacts of climate change.

Trade is a key mechanism for improving access to inputs such as fertilizers and machinery, but it is often constrained by a range of tariffs and nontariff measures. For example, fertilizer application rates are substantially lower in Africa than in other parts of the world. Farmers in Africa, especially in landlocked low- and middle-income countries, face higher prices for fertilizers than farmers elsewhere in the world, and markets in many African countries are too small to exploit scale economies linked to fertilizer production and even fertilizer blending. Part of the reason that regional fertilizer markets have not emerged is that individual countries prefer to specify their own fertilizer blends and specialty products. Hence, fertilizers cannot move freely from country to country. Regional markets with common fertilizer specifications could generate substantially lower prices. The lack of an effective system of standards is a major barrier to cross-border trade and regional fertilizer markets. Two key issues need to be addressed: (a) establishing a consistent and stable policy environment for regional trade in fertilizers and (b) investing in institutions that lower the transaction costs of coordination failures. Many countries have enacted new fertilizer laws in recent years, but few have also provided the resources to define and enforce regulations through standards and testing. Reducing the regulatory burden on fertilizers would increase their use, substantially raising farmers' economic returns and strengthening their ability to adapt to changing climatic conditions.

Adaptation can also take place through the application of new techniques and technologies. For example, planting seeds earlier can avoid extreme heat during the critical flowering stage. Access to new inputs that increase resilience to climate change (such as drought-resistant seeds and pesticides for weed control) is of particular importance. For low-income countries, trade is a key conduit for gaining knowledge and access to new technologies. But trade barriers often deny farmers access to higher-yielding seeds that are readily available elsewhere. Sanitary, phytosanitary, and plant quarantine measures, seed certification, and variety release regulations differ across regions and countries, creating barriers to the cross-border movement of seeds. In Africa, a lack of agreement on standards among agencies in different countries and inconsistent and heavy-handed application of control procedures for imports have hindered regional trade in seeds. Border customs officials who are not trained to understand seed trade policy exacerbate these costs and delays. As a result, seeds can be held up at borders for a long time, often rendering them useless. In some African countries, it can take two to three years for new seed varieties to be released, even if they are being used elsewhere on the continent. These delays reduce yields and productivity and are becoming more problematic as the climate changes.[1]

New technologies to adapt to climate change will typically require knowledge and guidance to ensure that they are applied in accordance with local conditions. The impact on productivity of investments in agricultural research and development (R&D) leading to new technologies depends on their uptake by farmers. Uptake can be challenging in low- and middle-income countries, where farmers are often heterogeneous, highly dispersed smallholders. The available evidence suggests that the impact of agricultural R&D on productivity is considerably lower in Africa than in other regions (Fuglie 2018). Access to extension services can facilitate the uptake of new seed varieties, for example, and will therefore be a critical element of adaptation to climate change in agriculture. Previous analysis has highlighted the potential to expand access to extension services by improving the cross-border mobility of extension service providers across Africa. Measures such as creating a regional database of agricultural specialists, removing barriers to movement derived from economic needs tests or lengthy administrative procedures to obtain a work permit,[2] as well as introducing transparent procedures to recognize the qualifications of agricultural specialists (such as mutual recognition agreements of professional qualifications) could improve cross-border mobility (World Bank 2012).

Adaptation mechanisms may work differently in low-income countries than in middle-income ones. For example, Cattaneo and Peri (2015) find that past temperature increases resulted in internal migration to urban areas and emigration abroad in middle-income countries but reduced the probability of leaving rural areas in poor countries. In the former, migration can provide an important mechanism of adjustment to climate change. However, in poor economies, lower agricultural productivity in rural areas (made worse by climate change) exacerbates the liquidity constraints to movement. As such, it is increasingly important to understand how climate change may affect agricultural trade flows and how low-income countries can address the impacts of climate change on them.

Access to environmental goods and services will be essential in the transition to a low-carbon global economy. Environmental goods and services can cover a range of areas, including air pollution control, renewable energy, water and waste management, environmental monitoring, assessment, and analysis, environmental consulting, remediation and clean-up services, cleaner technologies, and carbon capture and storage. As discussed in previous chapters, emerging emitters will be important drivers of higher emissions in the coming years, and the use of low-carbon technologies in low- and middle-income countries could reduce emissions by about 600 million tons of carbon dioxide (CO_2) by 2040, close to 10 percent of these countries' total emissions by that time. Few countries, if any, have the resources, technology, and expertise needed to convert to a low-carbon economy. Trade will thus play a vital role in the global diffusion of low-carbon technologies by giving countries access to a wider range of lower-cost environmental goods and services. This access will, in turn, create new business and job opportunities in areas that use, distribute, and maintain these new technologies.

Trade in environmental goods

Environmental goods are, simply put, those whose main function is to address or contribute to solving an environmental issue or challenge. Nearly 20 years ago, the World Trade Organization (WTO) launched negotiations on liberalizing trade in environmental goods and services under the Doha Round. The idea was to lower the costs of acquiring and using environmental technologies to combat a range of environmental problems, including climate change. Low- and middle-income countries could gain better access to markets for green goods and acquire green technology more easily and cheaply. These negotiations were held to liberalize trade, promote development, and better preserve the environment, leading some to label the Doha Round as a potential triple win (de Melo and Solleder 2020b, among others). A fourth possible win would be to avoid a clash between two global legal systems—the WTO rules and the emerging global rules for environmental protection, including the Sustainable Development Agenda of the United Nations, established in 2015, and the Paris Agreement, signed in 2016.

The stalemate of the Doha Round has prevented a global agreement on trade and the environment. A group of mainly high-income WTO members have instead negotiated a plurilateral agreement,[3] the Environmental Goods Agreement (EGA). The EGA is linked to the WTO framework because, as a plurilateral agreement, the liberalization of trade measures—through tariff cuts and other means—would be extended to all WTO members if a "critical mass" (say 85–90 percent of world trade in the concerned goods) is reached. The parties had hoped to finalize negotiations during the last negotiating round, which took place on December 3–4, 2016, with a view to wrapping up the talks in 2017. However, they failed to reach agreement on what constitutes a green good. Since then, plurilateral negotiations have not resumed.[4] Nevertheless, green liberalization is likely to resurface in a new round of plurilateral negotiations and in regional and bilateral trade agreements. Could low- and middle-income countries, including poor countries, benefit from some form of green-trade liberalization?

A critical issue for the liberalization of tariffs on green goods is how these goods are defined in trade classifications. For example, one commonly used list includes mainly industrial products—the Asia-Pacific Economic Cooperation (APEC) list—while a second list adds "environmentally preferable" products (EPPs)—that is, products produced in ways that are less detrimental to the environment, such as organic cotton. In talks held in the WTO Committee on Trade and Environment, Brazil has pushed to categorize biofuels as a green good, but many industrial countries, many of them European Union (EU) members, have not wanted to include agriculture in the trade and environment discussions and negotiations.

Recent amendments to the trade classification system (to be implemented in 2022) will help to improve data tracking of trade in environmental goods and related products. Amendments by the World Customs Organization to the Harmonized System nomenclature for classifying goods have made significant strides in classifying environmental goods. Many of the changes will facilitate the monitoring of exports and imports of environmentally sensitive products, such as electronic waste, but also trade in environmental goods, such as solar photovoltaic panels and mass spectrometers. However, Steenblik (2020) finds that, while this progress is significant, specific, harmonized codes are needed for the critical environmental goods that are increasingly emerging.

In general, tariffs on environmental goods are relatively low, with important exceptions for certain products and countries. Figure B.1 (appendix B) shows the latest information on the average most-favored-nation tariff for the APEC list of environmental goods.[5] A few island states levy very high tariffs of 20 percent or more. Of the larger low- and middle-income economies, Argentina, Brazil, Ethiopia, and the Central African Economic and Monetary Community (CEMAC) countries have average tariffs on environmental goods above 10 percent, although there is considerable variability across countries. Brazil, for example, levies a 14 percent tariff on blades and hubs, which are integral components of wind turbines. By contrast, Ethiopia has a 0 percent duty on these products. There are 24 countries with a tariff of 5 percent or more on solar photovoltaic cells and panels. Nevertheless, most countries have average tariffs on environmental goods of less than 5 percent, the average across all countries being 4.05 percent. There has been a modest reduction in such tariffs over the past two decades, with the global average at 5.69 percent in 2000. Reductions have been substantial in countries such as China, where average tariffs on environmental goods fell from 12.5 percent in 2000 to 4.6 percent in 2018. In Kenya, the decline has been even more pronounced—from 11.2 percent in 2000 to 0.66 percent in 2018. A few countries, including some low- and middle-income countries, have removed all tariffs on their imports of environmental goods. Among these countries are Japan, Mauritius, Papua New Guinea, Peru, and Switzerland.

Further global negotiations on tariffs on green goods will be challenging if only products on the APEC list are considered. On average, tariffs are low, especially in richer countries, and there is little improved market access to be achieved through global negotiations. Moreover, tariffs vary widely across low- and middle-income countries—from zero to relatively high tariffs—and there is no clear position on this limited list of goods. To move forward, countries could be encouraged to remove "nuisance tariffs" on environmental goods unilaterally (de Melo and Solleder 2019). Nuisance tariffs are tariff levels for which it is safe to assume that the cost of collection exceeds the amount of revenue generated. If tariffs of 5 percent or less were deemed to be nuisance tariffs in the case of environmental goods, their removal would affect about 45 percent of the flow of environmental goods trade in 2018.[6] The removal of nuisance tariffs would lead to about 75 percent of the flow of environmental goods being tariff-free. The remaining tariffs above 5 percent would be concentrated in a relatively small number of countries (figure 4.1). In 2018, a total of 78 countries had one or more tariffs on environmental goods above 5 percent, but, for 53 of these countries, the number of goods was merely 10 or fewer. Just 20 countries account for three-quarters of the tariffs above 5 percent.[7] Hence, bilateral dialogue and discussions with development and trading partners should be prioritized, in parallel with multilateral negotiations. Empirical studies tend to confirm the limited gains from tariff liberalization of goods on the APEC list of environmental goods (de Melo and Solleder 2020a; Tamini and Sorgho 2018, among others).

The barriers to trade in environmental goods are mostly nontariff barriers, and eliminating them should be a top priority. These barriers vary by country, but they mostly include technical barriers to trade and sanitary and phytosanitary measures—regulations that are put in place for many reasons, including health, safety, and environmental protection. The ambiguity in the application of these regulations can be exploited for trade-restrictive purposes. Other nontariff barriers include local-content requirements, specifically requirements that incentivize the use of locally sourced materials, cumbersome certification and licensing procedures, and price controls. Addressing these nontariff barriers by monitoring them closely and eliminating them will be fundamentally important to facilitating environmental goods trade. Already, several regional trade blocs have mechanisms for monitoring nontariff barriers, but these platforms do not differentiate between those that affect environmental goods and those that do not. Distinguishing the two would make for better data analysis and thus appropriate design of policy reform.

Trade in environmentally preferable products

Progress at the multilateral level in two areas could help to improve access to goods that contribute to lower carbon emissions and where low- and middle-income countries are likely to have strong interests: (1) expanding the range of environmental goods and (2) addressing nontariff barriers to trade in environmental goods. Several studies suggest that countries have a stronger interest when green liberalization includes EPPs (de Melo and Solleder 2020a, among others).

Environmentally preferable products or services are those that have less adverse impacts on human health and the environment than competing products or services designed to achieve the same purpose. These environmental benefits can arise in production, consumption, and disposal. EPPs of interest to low- and middle-income countries include a range of agricultural and natural products, including lac, gum, and resins; fertilizers, colorants, and wood products; wool, cotton, and silk; and vegetable fibers.

Governments, especially those of high-income countries, are often the largest purchasers of environmental goods and services and EPPs. In the United States, the federal government is the single largest purchaser of environmentally sustainable products and services, spending more than US$550 billion each year (EPA 2021). Hence, governments have substantial power to drive the growth of sustainable production. Ensuring that low- and middle-income countries that are efficient producers of environmental goods and EPPs have access to these markets could be instrumental not

FIGURE 4.1 Number of Environmental Goods with Tariffs above 5 Percent, 2018

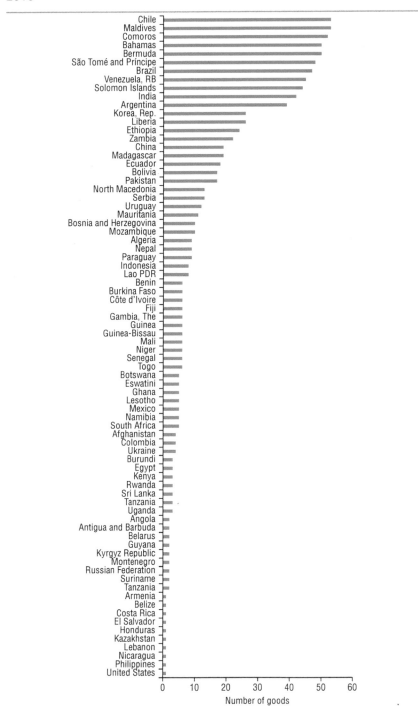

Source: World Bank calculations using data from World Integrated Trade Solutions.

only in achieving domestic environmental objectives but also in promoting sustainable development globally.

Tariffs are, on average, higher for EPPs. The global average was 7.3 percent in 2018.[8] But tariffs in the richer countries are relatively low—2.8 percent in Japan, 2.9 percent in the United States, and 3.4 percent in the EU (figure B.2 in appendix B). Further, low-income countries can access these markets at lower duties or duty-free under unilateral preference programs, such as the EU's Everything But Arms (EBA), the African Growth and Opportunity Act (AGOA) of the United States, and the Generalized System of Preferences (GSP) applied by many high-income countries.[9] Many of the gains from liberalizing trade in EPPs would thus come from trade between low- and middle-income countries. Therefore, these countries could improve their access to EPPs and contribute to their environmental objectives as well as boost trade with other low- and middle-income countries.

However, trade in both environmental goods and EPPs often requires agreement on sustainability criteria and standards. Countries that cannot provide traceability in the value chain and the necessary trading infrastructure, such as certification and inspection services to ensure that the product is genuinely environmentally preferable, may be excluded from overseas markets even if they are competitive in the sustainable production of the good—for example, tracing organic cotton to verify that it was produced according to relevant standards for organic produce and is not mixed with conventional cotton. Baltzer and Jensen (2015) argue that low-income countries may want to join the EGA negotiations if the latter become a forum for developing standards and sustainability criteria. Doing so would help to ensure that such standards are set relative to the reality of production in low- and middle-income countries and do not become a barrier to trade.

Nontariff measures on environmental goods and EPPs tend to be more prevalent in high-income than in low-income countries, reflecting underlying regulatory requirements. These requirements can easily become barriers to trade, especially for low- and middle-income countries. For example, testing and conformity assessment procedures are often lengthy and more costly for importers than for domestic firms and thus restrict trade in practice (de Melo and Solleder 2020a). Such measures tend to be particularly burdensome for low- and middle-income countries, whose exporters tend to be smaller and less able to absorb these additional costs. Local-content requirements can also be important barriers to trade in environmental goods.

These kinds of barriers can be reduced in various way, depending on the technical capacity of conformity assessment bodies, their accreditation, and the level of trust in regulatory systems. An important first step is simply to be transparent and exchange information, which builds confidence and trust and reduces transaction costs. One way to remove the barriers created by duplicative inspection, testing, and certification and lengthy approval procedures in the importing country is through mutual recognition of *accreditation systems and testing procedures*. In this way, exporters can assess conformity in domestic or regional laboratories before goods are exported and provide the information to authorities in the importing country. A next step is mutual recognition of conformity assessment *results*. The most advanced agreements relate to mutual recognition (or acceptance of equivalence) of technical regulations and harmonization of technical regulations and conformity assessment procedures. These various steps for removing the nontariff barriers associated with technical and sustainability standards can be pursued bilaterally, through regional integration agreements, and at the global level (through the WTO).

The EGA has been suggested as an appropriate forum for discussing and developing a plurilateral mutual recognition agreement for environmental goods (Sugathan 2018). Governments could come together at the WTO under the EGA and, starting with a few priority products for low- and middle-income countries, share information, explore common specifications and standards, and mutually recognize conformity assessment procedures. This effort could be backed up by a package of technical assistance and capacity building to help low- and middle-income countries implement traceability and testing and inspection services. Once these capacities have reached a suitable level, testing and inspection would be accepted as part of mutual recognition provisions.

Trade in environmental services

Trade in environmental services is often closely related and, in many cases, is integrated with trade in environmental goods. Access to trade in environmental services may be essential for the effective transfer and implementation of low-carbon technologies. But environmental services are not part of the discussions of trade in environmental goods under the EGA at the WTO. A mechanism is needed to bring together discussions of trade in environmental *goods* and trade in environmental *services*. Regarding the transition to a low-carbon economy, a wide range of environmental services are relevant, including those related to the construction, operation, and maintenance of renewable energy generation and distribution; advisory services on reducing tailpipe emissions from vehicles; application of clean technologies in manufacturing; advisory services on land-use management and agricultural practices; and services related to the inspection, certification, and testing of products and services produced with low-carbon technologies.

However, many of these services are not easily categorized under the existing structure of United Nations Central Product Classification (CPC), which typically forms the basis for discussions and negotiations at the WTO.[10] Several proposals have been developed for establishing more useful classifications. Steenblik and Nordås (2021) make a significant contribution by listing and describing specific environmental services, classified according to United Nations CPC Version 2.1, using ex-outs where necessary.[11] Their study identifies more than 65 possible categories of environmental services at the subclass or ex-out level. A new category of environmental services for climate change mitigation may be one option to avoid some of the challenges that have bogged down negotiations about other environmental services, such as those related to water and waste management. Another factor hindering negotiations is the lack of information and indicators on the restrictiveness of policies affecting trade in environmental services. Nevertheless, there is plenty of scope for progress within limited boundaries of services that can be linked directly to climate change mitigation and adaptation and within the main modes of delivery: commercial presence and movement of persons.

Anecdotal evidence supports the view that environmental goods and services are complementary. Based on interviews conducted with companies selling or purchasing environmental products, Sweden's National Board of Trade concluded that some services were "indispensable for the trade in environmental goods" and went on to advocate the joint liberalization of trade in environmental goods and associated services, given their "synergetic relationship." The US International Trade Commission arrived at similar findings for the solar, wind, small hydropower, and geothermal sectors, stressing that "a broad group of services are indispensable to the development and functioning of renewable energy projects" (Sauvage and Timiliotis 2017). If environmental goods are the hardware for addressing climate change, environmental services are the software that ensures they work as intended (Steenblik and Droege 2019).

As is the case with many capital goods, the installation and operation of machines and pieces of equipment to prevent or abate pollution can be complex, requiring specific user knowledge and skills that can be costly to acquire. Demand for such knowledge and skills tends to be strong in the environmental sector, where products often lie toward the top of the complexity ladder. A consequence of this complexity is that consumers do not value wind turbines, solar photovoltaics, or gas chromatographs per se. Rather, they seek to acquire these goods in combination with ancillary services such as installation, technical support, training, and maintenance. Therefore, any policy restriction placed on the provision of those ancillary services has the potential to deter or slow down the uptake of cleaner technologies (Sauvage 2014).

Restrictions on trade in services have a detrimental effect on the international activities of firms providing environmental consulting and engineering services. These kinds of services feed into numerous projects spanning all sorts of environmental domains, from renewable energy to water treatment and noise abatement. Restricting the supply of these services therefore makes the diffusion of cleaner technologies and practices unnecessarily costly (OECD 2017). Just as trade in environmental *goods* has helped to lower the price of cleaner equipment and technologies, trade in environmental *services* could make the prevention and control of pollution cheaper by allowing firms to source the services they need from foreign suppliers. Trade restrictions on services increase the project costs associated with environmental aspects. Access to information and communication services plays an important role in the transfer and implementation of new environmental technologies (UNCTAD 2021, 36).

Although the past two decades have witnessed several initiatives aimed at liberalizing trade in environmental goods and services, progress has been dismal. The EGA is essentially concerned with environmental goods, leaving the issue of environmental services by and large unaddressed. Where environmental services have been liberalized, liberalization was more the accidental result of broader trade negotiations that were not intended to remove impediments to the diffusion of cleaner technologies. The neglect of environmental services goes beyond trade negotiations, generally affecting discourse on the trade-environment nexus. A similar picture emerges on the analytical front, as most studies to date have concentrated on environmental goods rather than services, a key reason being the lack of data for empirically analyzing trade in environmental services and even trade in services more generally (OECD 2017, 14).[12]

Nonetheless, not all hope is lost for the liberalization of environmental services, as structured discussions are taking place on trade and environmental sustainability at the WTO (for more information, see WTO 2020). A smaller group of countries, led by New Zealand—Costa Rica, Fiji, Iceland, and Norway—together with Switzerland have launched a new initiative: the Agreement on Climate Change, Trade, and Sustainability (ACCTS). The agreement aims to generate momentum for developing wider, globally agreed-on solutions to environmental challenges. The countries involved plan to slash barriers to trade in environmental goods and services, phase out their fossil fuel subsidies, and encourage the promotion and application of voluntary eco-labeling programs and mechanisms. These countries envisage ACCTS as a "living agreement" that can be updated and take on additional issues as needed. ACCTS could serve as a trailblazer agreement that other WTO members could join once they meet the required commitments and disciplines. Starting the initiative on a small scale was a deliberate choice, although other members will be welcome to join at a later stage. The ACCTS countries plan to extend their concessions on environmental goods and services to all WTO members on a most-favored-nation basis and have agreed to dispense with the critical-mass requirement. The latter is a landmark move in trade rulemaking, which shows the group's commitment to achieving positive environmental outcomes, not just improving export opportunities (Steenblik and Droege 2019).

Compared with other service sectors (such as tourism, financial services, and telecommunications), the level of environmental service commitments bound under the General Agreement on Trade in Services (GATS) is modest.[13] Many countries have made no commitments at all under mode 1, meaning that mode 1 is "unbound" in terms of both market access and national treatment (table 4.1).[14] This trend is less pronounced for the other three modes of supply, but remains significant nonetheless (Sauvage and Timiliotis 2017, 15). In the environmental services sector, most trade takes place through commercial presence (mode 3), with the accompanying presence of natural persons (mode 4). Due to technological developments, cross-border supply (mode 1) is gaining importance. The limited commitments made by WTO member states under GATS is attributable to several factors, chief among them (a) the prevailing role played by public entities in providing environmental services and (b) the propensity of environmental services to become natural monopolies (special distribution or collection networks, high capital investments) (APEC 2020).[15]

Nevertheless, much liberalization seems to have taken place in the context of regional trade agreements. In 2009 the Organisation for Economic Co-operation and Development (OECD) conducted a survey of the preferential content of services in regional trade agreements, finding that roughly 40 percent of all market-access commitments for environmental services in the regional trade agreements surveyed were GATS-plus, meaning that they improved on prior GATS commitments. A similar analysis undertaken by de Melo and Vijil (2014) finds that regional trade agreements have tended to improve on GATS commitments made under environmental

TABLE 4.1   GATS Commitments for Environmental Services, by Supply Mode
Percentage

Mode of supply	Market access		National treatment	
	Unbound	Full commitment	Unbound	Full treatment
Mode 1: Cross-border	84	10	80	20
Mode 2: Consumption abroad	57	32	55	45
Mode 3: Commercial presence	55	20	55	45
Mode 4: Movement of natural persons	54	0	54	14

Source: Sauvage and Timiliotis 2017, 15.
Note: GATS = General Agreement on Trade in Services. The data refer to the sample of World Trade Organization (WTO) members covered by Miroudot, Sauvage, and Sudreau (2010), which includes all Organisation for Economic Co-operation and Development (OECD) members and a large number of nonmember economies, including Albania, China, Costa Rica, Croatia, El Salvador, Honduras, India, Indonesia, Jamaica, Jordan, Malaysia, Morocco, Oman, Peru, the Philippines, Singapore, Thailand, and Vietnam. The European Union, being a customs union, is treated here as a single WTO member. Environmental services refer to activities 6A, 6B, 6C, and 6D in the Sectoral Classification List (W/120).

services, particularly in the case of North-South regional trade agreements. This finding partly reflects the larger number of commitments that high-income countries have made in GATS, which has left little "binding overhang" or "GATS water" to be addressed through regional trade agreements between high-income countries (OECD 2017, 14).

Conclusions

Access to environmental goods and services will play a critical role in mitigating emissions and achieving the Paris Agreement commitments, as well as in adapting to a changing environment. The following are among the key issues:

- *Reviewing tariffs on environmental goods,* especially in low- and middle-income countries, to ensure that they are consistent with environmental objectives

- *Identifying and quantifying the main nontariff barriers to trade in environmental goods* and opportunities as the basis for regulatory streamlining and cooperation at the regional and global levels; enhanced streamlining and cooperation would reduce trade costs for these products through mutual recognition of testing and conformity assessment, equivalence, or harmonization

- *Improving access to environmental services through trade,* which is essential to realizing the gains from trade in environmental goods, as these elements are complementary in implementation; improving access will require efforts at both the regional level and at the WTO to agree on definitions of environmental services and identify the main trade-restricting barriers and mechanisms for monitoring the effective implementation of commitments.

Better access to environmentally preferable products offers additional opportunities to mitigate carbon emissions. The ability to verify the environmental characteristics of the production of goods will become increasingly important for firms that supply consumers directly. This trend will be strengthened further by the fact that end users are becoming more aware of the impacts of their consumption and that buyers in overseas markets and multinational firms are increasingly seeking to reduce carbon emissions along their supply chains (chapter 4). The following are some of the key issues in this context:

- Reducing the much higher tariffs on categories of goods in which low- and middle-income countries have opportunities to supply EPPs

- Distinguishing EPPs in standard trade classifications and addressing traceability and the ability to demonstrate carbon competitiveness

- Accounting for the important role that government procurement plays in the market for EPPs.

Notes

1. In Ethiopia, for example, the use of improved hybrid maize could help to quadruple productivity (Alemu 2010).

2. An *economic needs test* conditions market access on meeting certain economic criteria.

3. A *plurilateral* agreement implies that WTO member countries would be given the choice to agree to new rules on a voluntary basis. This contrasts with a *multilateral* WTO agreement, where all WTO members are party to the agreement.

4. A group of 53 WTO members—including Chad, Chile, Mexico, and Senegal—have recently initiated structured discussions on trade and environmental sustainability. The objective of these discussions is "to collaborate, prioritize, and advance discussions on trade and environmental sustainability," including climate change. Initial steps have included sharing best practices and lessons learned, along with examining the need for technical assistance and capacity building. While some countries have submitted proposals for discussion topics, with the liberalization of environmental goods and services figuring heavily, future work remains to be defined. See IISD (2021).

5. The *most-favored-nation* tariff is applied to all WTO members under nondiscriminatory trade policy. Lower tariffs may be applied to countries with which there is a preferential trade agreement.

6. Determined in this context by the number of countries reporting tariffs in 2018 and the number of environmental goods on the APEC list; countries in a customs union are counted individually.

7. The inclusion of Chile distorts the picture somewhat, as the country has a common tariff of 6 percent for all the 53 lines.

8. This report uses the list of EPPs defined by Zugravu-Soilita (2018).

9. The EBA program removes tariffs and quotas for all imports of goods (except arms and ammunition) into the EU from low-income countries. AGOA provides trade preferences for quotas and duty-free entry into the United States for certain goods from eligible African countries, expanding the benefits under the GSP.

10. The Sectoral Classification List (W/120)—linked to the 1991 version of the United Nations CPC—includes just four categories, which are now out of date. Existing categories that directly identify environmental services are limited to (1) sewage and waste collection, treatment and disposal, and other environmental protection services; (2) services furnished by environmental advocacy groups; (3) studies of environmental impact and economic assessments of urban development plans; and (4) environmental consulting services.

11. "Ex-outs" describe specific services or service categories that are not fully identified by the United Nations CPC list and are instead captured by national programs that may vary from country to country.

12. Information on barriers to services trade was also scarce until the 2014 release of the Services Trade Restrictiveness Index, which looks at more than 10,000 individual regulations to identify policy measures that inhibit services trade in sectors such as accounting, engineering, and telecommunications. However, numerous challenges make it difficult to quantitatively assess the impacts that current policies have had on trade in environmental services, among others, and the question of how to define the scope of those services (OECD 2017, 14).

13. See WTO, "Environmental Services," https://www.wto.org/english/tratop_e/serv_e/environment_e/environment_e.htm.

14. "Unbound" indicates an absence of constraint or obligation. When a mode of supply is listed as "unbound" in the market access or national treatment column, a new measure that is inconsistent with market access and national treatment may be introduced in the future.

15. See WTO, "Environmental Services," https://www.wto.org/english/tratop_e/serv_e/environment_e/environment_e.htm); OECD (2017, 12).

References

Alemu, Dawit. 2010. "The Political Economy of Ethiopian Cereal Seed Systems: State Control, Market Liberalisation and Decentralisation." Future Agricultures Working Paper 17, Future Agricultures Consortium, Brighton, UK.

APEC (Asia-Pacific Economic Cooperation). 2020. "Trade in Environmental Services: A WTO Perspective." Presentation at the workshop "Manufacturing-Related Services and Environmental Services—Contribution to the Final Review of Manufacturing-Related Services Action Plan and Environmental Services Action Plan, August 19, 2020." Agenda: 11ii 2020/GOS/WKSP3/010, APEC Malaysia, August 19.

Baltzer, K., and H. Jensen. 2015. "Study of the Impacts of Green Trade Liberalisation on Least Developed Countries." Ministry of Foreign Affairs of Denmark, Copenhagen. https://um.dk/en/danidaen/partners/research/other//~/media/um/english-site/documents/danida/partners/researchorg/research-studies/green%20trade%20final%20report%20november%202015.pdf.

Cattaneo, Cristina, and Giovanni Peri. 2015. "The Migration Response to Increasing Temperatures." NBER Working Paper 21622, National Bureau of Economic Research, Cambridge, MA.

de Melo, Jaime, and Jean-Marc Solleder. 2019. "Reviving the Environmental Goods Agreement: Why It Matters, Why It Is Stalled, and How to Move Forward." Yale University, New Haven, CT.

de Melo, Jaime, and Jean-Marc Solleder. 2020a. "Barriers to Trade in Environmental Goods: How Important They Are and What Should Developing Countries Expect from Their Removal." *World Development* 130 (June): 104910.

de Melo, Jaime, and Jean-Marc Solleder. 2020b. "The EGA Negotiations: Why They Are Important, Why They Are Stalled, and Challenges Ahead." *Journal of World Trade* 54 (3): 333–47.

de Melo, Jaime, and Mariana Vijil. 2014. "Barriers to Trade in Environmental Goods and Services: How Important Are They? How Much Progress at Reducing Them?" CEPR Discussion Paper DP9869, Centre for Economic Policy Research, London.

EPA (Environmental Protection Agency). 2021. "Sustainable Marketplace: Greener Products and Services; Recommendations of Specifications, Standards, and Ecolabels for Federal Purchasing." US EPA, Washington, DC. https://www.epa.gov/greenerproducts/recommendations-specifications-standards-and-ecolabels-federal-purchasing.

Fuglie, Keith. 2018. "R&D Capital, R&D Spillovers, and Productivity Growth in World Agriculture." *Applied Economic Perspectives and Policy* 40 (3): 421–44.

Gouel, Christophe, and David Laborde. 2018. "The Crucial Role of International Trade in Adaptation to Climate Change." NBER Working Paper 25221, National Bureau of Economic Research, Cambridge, MA.

IISD (International Institute for Sustainable Development). 2021. "Trade and Environment Structured Discussions among WTO Member Group Get Underway." SDG Knowledge Hub, March 10. http://sdg.iisd.org/commentary/policy-briefs/trade-and-environment-structured-discussions-among-wto-member-group-get-underway.

Miroudot, S., J. Sauvage, and M. Sudreau. 2010. "Multilateralising Regionalism: How Preferential Are Services Commitments in Regional Trade Agreements?" OECD Trade Policy Papers, No. 106, OECD Publishing, Paris, https://doi.org/10.1787/5km362n24t8n-en.

OECD (Organisation for Economic Co-operation and Development). 2017. "Trade in Services Related to the Environment." COM/TAD/ENV/JWPTE(2015)61/FINAL 27-Mar-2017, OECD Joint Working Party on Trade and Environment, Paris.

Sauvage, Jehan. 2014. "The Stringency of Environmental Regulations and Trade in Environmental Goods." OECD Trade and Environment Working Paper, Organisation for Economic Co-operation and Development, Paris. 10.1787/5jxrjn7xsnmq-en.

Sauvage, Jehan, and Christina Timiliotis. 2017. "Joint Working Party on Trade and Environment: Trade in Services Related to the Environment." COM/TAD/ENV/JWPTE (2015) 61 /FINAL. Organisation for Economic Co-operation and Development, Paris.

Steenblik, Ronald P. 2020. "Code Shift: The Environmental Significance of the 2022 Amendments to the Harmonized System." International Institute for Sustainable Development, Geneva.

Steenblik, Ronald, and Susanne Droege. 2019. "Time to ACCTS? Five Countries Announce New Initiative on Trade and Climate Change." International Institute for Sustainable Development, Geneva. https://www.iisd.org/articles/time-accts-five-countries-announce -new-initiative-trade-and-climate-change.

Steenblik, Ronald, and Hildegunn Nordås. 2021. "Environmental Services in the APEC Region: Definition, Challenges, and Opportunities." APEC#221-CT-01.8, May 2021, Committee on Trade and Investment (CTI), Group on Services (GOS), Asia-Pacific Economic Cooperation, Singapore. https://www.apec.org/Publications/2021/05 /Environmental-Services-in-the-APEC-Region.

Sugathan, Mahesh. 2018. "Mutual Recognition Agreement on Conformity Assessment: A Deliverable on Non-Tariff Measures in the EGA." Issue Paper 21, International Centre for Trade and Sustainable Development, Geneva.

Tamini, Lota, and Zakaria Sorgho. 2018. "Trade in Environmental Goods: Evidences from an Analysis Using Elasticities of Trade Costs." *Environmental and Resource Economics* 70 (1): 53–75.

UNCTAD (United Nations Conference on Trade and Development). 2021. *Trade and Environment Review 2021: Trade Climate Readiness for Developing Countries.* Geneva: United Nations.

World Bank. 2012. *Africa Can Help Feed Africa.* Washington, DC: World Bank.

WTO (World Trade Organization). 2020. "New Initiatives Launched to Intensify WTO Work on Trade and the Environment." WTO, Geneva. https://www.wto.org/english/news_e /news20_e/envir_17nov20_e.htm.

Zugravu-Soilita, Natalia. 2018. "The Impact of Trade in Environmental Goods on Pollution: What Are We Learning from the Transition Economies' Experience?" *Environmental Economics and Policy Studies* 20 (4): 785–827.

5

Environmental Policies and Trade

Given the lack of a global agreement on specific economic measures to reduce carbon emissions, both policy makers and the private sector are under increasing pressure to introduce measures that will reduce their country's or company's carbon footprint. This chapter reviews emerging measures and assesses their implications for trade flows, especially those of low-income countries.

The Carbon Border Adjustment Mechanism and low-income-country trade

The Paris Agreement allows countries to work from highly different starting points and with different ambitions toward the common goal of achieving zero net emissions. While the agreement is aimed at global convergence of mitigation efforts, in the first years of implementation, different starting points and ambitions entail both variety and asymmetry in the use of mitigation instruments. Firms in countries with high ambitions for mitigation fear an erosion of competitiveness under this scenario. Steelmakers in the European Union (EU), for example, must buy emissions allowances in the EU Emissions Trading System (ETS);[1] if the price of these allowances becomes significant, steelmakers fear that they will be unable to compete with steelmakers in countries not subject to such costly carbon regulation. As a result, there is a risk that production may shift to unregulated countries.

This concern over a loss of competitiveness without an accompanying gain in the global fight against climate change intersects with the concerns that environmentalists have about carbon leakage. Carbon leakage occurs when carbon emissions rise in countries with weak carbon regulations because stricter regulations in other countries make unregulated markets more attractive and competitive. So far, there is no conclusive evidence to support this perceived risk.[2] Carbon border adjustments[3] are being explored as one solution to the problem of carbon leakage.[4] Such adjustments add a price to imports that corresponds to the price of carbon emissions that domestic firms pay. This adjustment is designed to nullify the cost advantage that firms producing in an unregulated country enjoy when selling in a regulated country. Border adjustment is often envisioned as a tax levied at the border, but it may also occur by other means;

for example, the EU has recently proposed that importers of certain carbon-intensive products covered by the EU ETS buy carbon emissions allowances. This approach would, in theory, have the same effect as levying a tax at the border.

Carbon border adjustments can be politically controversial, challenging to reconcile with international trade law, and administratively demanding to implement. A key concern is that carbon border taxes may be misused for protectionist purposes (Brenton, Edwards-Jones, and Jensen 2009; Messerlin 2012). For this reason, any new program will be carefully examined for its consistency with World Trade Organization (WTO) rules and is very likely to be challenged in the WTO dispute settlement system. Each new carbon border adjustment program will need to demonstrate that it correctly accounts for the carbon footprint of products, is flexible enough to allow exporters to demonstrate better performance, and takes account of carbon mitigation policies other than carbon-pricing mechanisms, among other requirements for complying with General Agreement on Tariffs and Trade (GATT) rules.[5] A further issue is the consistency of trade measures with the Paris Agreement and the principle of common but differentiated responsibility. More generally, consistency is needed between trade and environmental policies to ensure that resources are used both efficiently and sustainably, facilitating poverty reduction while mitigating climate change.

Practical considerations for establishing carbon border adjustment

The practical problems of implementing border adjustment are a major hurdle. They arise from the technical complexity of calculating carbon footprints. There is no easy and commonly accepted way to calculate the carbon footprint of a product arriving at the border. But this information is required to tax the embedded carbon, together with information on carbon taxes (if any) already levied on the product in the country of production. Supply chains are long and complex, with sources of carbon emissions entering at multiple points and with many possibilities of substitution occurring along the way. Aluminum, for example, has half the carbon footprint if produced from recycled as opposed to raw aluminum, and no customs officer can tell the difference. There is no broad consensus on how to calculate the carbon footprint of a product; several organizations have developed competing international standards, and data are often a problem.

Low- and middle-income countries have a stake in how future border adjustment programs address these practical problems. Common methodologies for calculating carbon content may be more difficult to apply in low-income countries, which may also face more severe data limitations. Commonly used standards for determining carbon footprint require many subjective choices to be made in the calculations and leave plenty of room to arrive at different estimates simply by varying plausible assumptions and using different yet respectable data sources (Brenton, Edwards-Jones, and Jensen 2010; Plassmann et al. 2010). Many carbon footprint analysts apply life cycle analysis to estimate carbon footprints, but subjective decisions need to be made regarding systems' boundaries (where the analysis should begin and end), the data on which to base carbon content calculations, and benchmarks to use if data are missing or a producing country is not willing to submit the necessary data.[6]

Regarding boundaries for the analysis, carbon reporting categorizes emissions in three groups: scope 1, scope 2, and scope 3. *Scope 1* emissions arise directly from owned or controlled sources, such as fuel combustion for onsite gas boilers and operation of company vehicles. *Scope 2* emissions are indirect emissions related to purchased energy, heat, steam, or cooling—for example, emissions from the operation of machinery using purchased electricity. *Scope 3* emissions are all other indirect emissions, including purchased inputs from external suppliers, employee commuting, business travel, waste management, distribution, energy used in consuming the product (for example, electricity used in boiling water for cooking vegetables), and so on.

Applying wide boundaries—for example, by including scope 3 emissions—makes for a more complete analysis and reveals a greater impact on emissions, but at the cost of complicating the calculations, enhancing the need for data, and increasing potential resistance to the chosen approach. Many low-income-country export commodities are traded in value chains without traceability, making it particularly hard to travel up the value chain to quantify all potential carbon sources. Other exports, like clothing and footwear, are traded through value chains where inputs are shifted frequently and the big brands procuring those exports often change suppliers.

To facilitate calculations, initial attempts to design a practical carbon border adjustment program are likely to include scope 1 and scope 2, but not scope 3, emissions. Emissions from transporting to market and from consumption to disposal of goods will probably also likely be excluded. Those that support the exclusion of scope 3 emissions often do so because they expect a program to cover mainly heavy industrial products, electricity and heating installation, and similar activities in which most of the carbon dioxide (CO_2) is emitted at the production site. For other products, like agricultural and light manufacturing goods, the largest share of emissions happens upstream in the value chain, especially in the consumption stage. However, if current emissions reduction policies and measures to achieve the 1.5°C target are increasingly enforced—for example, to give space to the emerging emitters to continue their development trajectory—the pressure to include scope 3 emissions in these programs may grow.

In general, the greater the use of benchmarks and readily available data (rather than tailor-made, product-specific data), the easier and less costly the calculations will be. But ease and economy may come at the cost of both incentives—and hence their impact on global emissions—and WTO legality. To give individual producers and importers an incentive to lower emissions, calculations must reflect the emissions of those individual firms. If the benchmark is crude—like industry averages—an individual firm may have no real incentive to lower emissions. Applying industrywide average emissions from the country of origin to imported products alleviates the difficulty of collecting emissions data in the exporting countries but may not capture the reality of production in those countries. Another approach that has been proposed is to base emissions on the best or worst available technology in use globally, which may be difficult to determine. In a practical example, EU product-specific benchmarks based on the 10 percent best-performing installations in the EU were established by the European Commission (EC) to implement the EU ETS. "Fairness," in the WTO sense, may require that foreign producers be allowed to demonstrate better-than-benchmark performance by submitting calculations of their products' actual carbon footprint.

An alternative approach to measurement that avoids some of the methodological difficulties inherent in applying life cycle analysis is the use of environmental input-output (IO) analysis. A growing number of multiregional IO databases contain detailed information on the carbon footprint of traded goods in different sectors and thus help to ease data limitations. This approach has the advantage of not requiring boundaries to be set. It is a top-down type of analysis in which detailed footprints are derived from aggregate IO data. By contrast, life cycle analysis is a bottom-up type of analysis where carbon footprints are calculated using finely granulated micro-level data. IO analysis is more relevant for a border adjustment program that requires rough sectoral carbon emissions data to levy carbon taxes corresponding to industry averages in either the importing country or the country of origin. But a border adjustment program that offers overseas producers the option to prove the actual carbon footprint of their product may be more effective in achieving its underlying objective of reducing emissions, which will require some form of life cycle analysis.

Studies of carbon border adjustment programs rarely take conditions in low-income countries into account, and indeed often appear unaware of them. It is unclear whether IO analysis really lessens methodological and data problems. Environmental IO analysis has rarely been applied in low-income countries, making data challenges very likely. Multiregional IO databases do not cover low-income countries sufficiently. Applying IO data derived from analyses of high-income and middle-income countries to low-income countries may severely misrepresent the nature of technology, production, and production links in these countries.

How carbon border adjustment might affect low-income-country export opportunities

In July 2021, the EC announced the details of the Carbon Border Adjustment Mechanism (CBAM) that will be part of the ambitious European Green Deal. This program will be the first to incorporate international border tax adjustments in climate policy.[7] The EC has provided initial details, but several issues regarding implementation will be confirmed after additional consultations (EC 2021). The deliberations of the EU have highlighted the key issues inherent in designing such programs. The EC has stressed that the program will comply with WTO rules and be implemented gradually, starting with selected sectors. Given the political, legal, and practical problems of designing and implementing the CBAM, the following are among the principles likely to be reflected in actual programs around the world and how they are being addressed in the EU proposal (EC 2021):

- *Scope of the program.* The program will initially be limited to carbon-intensive industrial products, most notably cement, electricity, fertilizers, aluminum, and iron and steel. Limiting the scope to known high-emitting products will make it easier to manage the program and more likely that it can be justified successfully under GATT Article XX. However, discussions are under way to broaden the scope and add downstream products and assembled products, such as cars, after 2030.

- *Special and differential treatment for low-income countries.* Somewhat surprisingly, while the EC proposal recognizes that preferential treatment for low-income countries is an "established procedure," that these countries currently account for a negligible share of EU imports of commodities covered by the CBAM, and that the CBAM could entail a disproportionate burden for them, there is no exemption for low-income countries. The EC argues that there is a risk that the CBAM will lead to higher emissions in low-income countries and seeks to avoid "new global dividing lines between countries with a low- and high-carbon export structure." It does suggest that there could be a gradual phasing in of the CBAM for existing production capacities in low-income countries. Instead, the EC proposes targeted support to poor countries for the transition to low-carbon production structures through technical assistance, technology transfer, capacity building, and financial support.

- *Lower duties (certificates required in the EU program) for trading partners with policies that raise the price of carbon.* Comparing the outcomes of different regulatory systems could be demanding, and it remains unclear how the grounds for exemptions could be evaluated.

- *Compatibility with WTO rules.* The program is more likely to be deemed compatible with WTO rules if

  - Imported products are not taxed higher than domestic products on a volume or per-unit basis. There is some concern that, when phasing in the CBAM, the EU will continue to provide free allowances to domestic firms, which could entail higher effective taxation of imports.

  - Exporters are allowed to demonstrate their actual carbon footprint. The EU proposal allows for production-specific calculation of embedded emissions.[8] Specific details remain to be defined, but the proposal provides considerable leeway for the EC to define key issues such as system boundaries and emission factors. It is unclear which standards and methodologies should be applied. Nevertheless, the data requirements will likely be challenging for firms in many low- and middle-income countries.

- *Practical implementation issues.* Practical implementation issues will entail border adjustment mechanisms that allow for readily available benchmarks—such as domestic industry averages and best or worst available technology—rather than carbon footprints measured at the product level. The EU proposal allows for default values where actual data on emissions cannot be calculated. These values will be calculated as the average emissions intensity of each exporting country, for each of the goods, *increased by a mark-up* determined by the EC. As noted, this approach risks taxing the most carbon-efficient producers more heavily than the least efficient ones and hence reducing the incentives to invest in low-carbon technologies. Further, under the EU proposal, if it is deemed that reliable data for the exporting country for a type of good are not available, then the default value will be based on the average emissions intensity of the 10 percent worst-performing EU installations for that type of good.[9]

- *Fair and transparent process.* The strong political interests in carbon border adjustment and the potential need to seek justification under GATT Article XX should ensure that the process for designing and implementing the CBAM is fair and transparent. Low-income countries have limited capacity to participate in such a process, so social and employment impact assessments will probably be needed. The EC has undertaken such an analysis, which briefly covers impacts on low-income countries.

The design of the CBAM will be critical in determining its impact on low- and middle-income countries. A recent detailed sector-level study of the potential impact of the EU's CBAM on India, Thailand, and Vietnam comes to the following conclusions:[10]

- The CBAM can have a very different impact, depending on its specific design.
- The choice of default CO_2 intensity values significantly influences impacts; box 5.1 illustrates this with the steel industry.
- Exporting-country CO_2 intensity is not always higher than EU intensity.
- At a specific product level, CBAM payments can represent a significant share of current prices (for example, up to 50 percent for cement).

BOX 5.1 CO_2 Intensity and Carbon Competitiveness in the Steel Industry

Steel production is currently highly emissive, but carbon intensities vary widely, depending on the production technology used. Figure B5.1.1 presents carbon dioxide (CO_2) intensity values related to the production of crude steel in the European Union (EU), India, Thailand, and Vietnam, based on the production technologies applied in each country and the energy source used. Thailand is carbon competitive and would be burdened unfairly by a border tax based on EU default values. Vietnam is carbon competitive if direct emissions are considered but less so if indirect emissions are included.

FIGURE B5.1.1 CO_2 Intensity Values for Steel

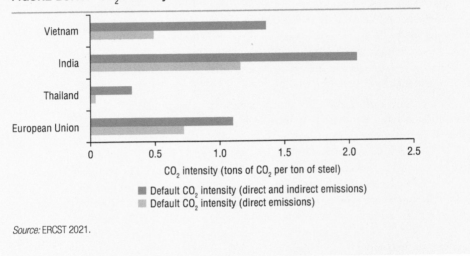

Source: ERCST 2021.

- Serious implementation problems are likely to arise because of limited data availability, especially in low- and middle-income countries.
- Default values should be product specific and change over time to reflect changing technology.
- It will be important to allow foreign producers to prove that their goods are "cleaner" than the default values associated with benchmark production processes.

Having a good understanding of the patterns of carbon emissions throughout the relevant value chains and access to carbon accounting and various services of verification will become a source of competitiveness. Many low- and middle-income countries have limited exports of the most carbon-intensive products and may not be affected immediately and directly by the EU's CBAM and other programs that may follow. Nevertheless, they may be affected indirectly—for example, if they export raw materials or intermediate inputs to countries that are subject to a carbon border adjustment tax and they import carbon-intensive products from countries that implement carbon regulation. Low-income countries may not be exempted from services; countries with a significant share of exports transported by air or with large tourism sectors would be affected if aviation becomes subject to carbon border adjustments. It is also possible that the EU's tightening of carbon regulation will lead EU importers and manufacturers to put pressure on their overseas suppliers of raw materials and inputs to reduce carbon emissions. Finally, while the EU program is initially limited to a small number of carbon-intensive products, the scope of the program may be extended, especially if the pilot program appears to be insufficient in meeting the EU's objective of reducing carbon emissions by 55 percent from 1990 levels by 2030. Hence, building the capacity to measure and verify carbon emissions will become increasingly important for producers throughout the world as programs to regulate carbon become more common and more expansive. In addition, as discussed below, private firms will be increasingly looking for suppliers that can demonstrate carbon competitiveness as part of their own corporate carbon management agenda.

Structural economic modeling using stylized scenarios of measures to achieve nationally determined contributions (NDCs) to the Paris Agreement and the bolder targets of the European Green Deal suggest that the impacts on most low-income countries will be limited.[11] Box 5.2 summarizes the modeling approach and policy scenarios, which are explored in more detail by Chepeliev et al. (2021).

BOX 5.2 Modeling the Impacts of Nationally Determined Contributions and Carbon Border Adjustments

The analysis presented here is based on a global, dynamic computable general equilibrium (CGE) model—the multiregional input-output (MRIO) version of the ENVISAGE model.[a] This approach allows for the analysis of global development and structural transformation, incorporating complex interactions of productivity differences at the country, sector, or factor level; shifts in demand as income changes; demographic and skill dynamics in factor markets; and changes in comparative advantages. It extends the standard modeling framework by incorporating MRIO tables that distinguish between imports of intermediate, final, and investment goods to better capture the nature of trade. The CGE model uses the Global Trade Analysis Project (GTAP) Version 10 database, with 2014 as the reference year, and is run until 2030. The analysis covers 27 sectors and 21 countries or regions.

The nationally determined contribution (NDC) targets are specified in the form of carbon dioxide (CO_2) emissions reduction in 2030 relative to levels in the pre-COVID baseline scenario. The model reflects the impact of COVID-19 on emissions trajectories. It is assumed that countries implement carbon-pricing policies to reach their NDC commitments, and the model estimates the carbon price consistent with achieving these targets. Corresponding 2030 carbon prices range from less than US$5 per ton of CO_2 in Sub-Saharan African countries, India, and Malaysia to more than US$30 per ton of CO_2 in Brazil, Turkey, the European Union (EU), and some other high-income countries.

In addition to the NDC targets, the model explores the more ambitious climate mitigation efforts of the EU Green Deal to cut emissions by 55 percent in 2030 relative to the 1990 level (EC 2019). This goal is achieved by a further increase in the price of carbon used in the model, together with the Carbon Border Adjustment Mechanism to prevent carbon leakage. The border adjustment takes the form of an ad valorem equivalent tax imposed on region- and commodity-specific carbon content of imports into the EU. The carbon price used to determine the border tax rate is estimated as the difference between the carbon price in the EU and the carbon price in the exporting country or region. The tax is based on the carbon content of the product in the exporting country and not on some measure of emissions in production in the EU. Border taxes are only levied on products from sectors covered by the EU Emissions Trading System.

a. ENVISAGE is a CGE model that assesses interactions between economies and the global environment and the way in which these interactions are affected by anthropogenic greenhouse gas emissions. It is designed to analyze a range of issues related to the economics of climate change (including baseline levels of CO_2 and greenhouse gases), the impact of climate change on the economy, adaptation to climate change, and distributional consequences of climate change.

FIGURE 5.1 Change in Real Income and Carbon Prices Associated with Achievement of Nationally Determined Contribution Targets in a Post-COVID Scenario, by Region, 2030

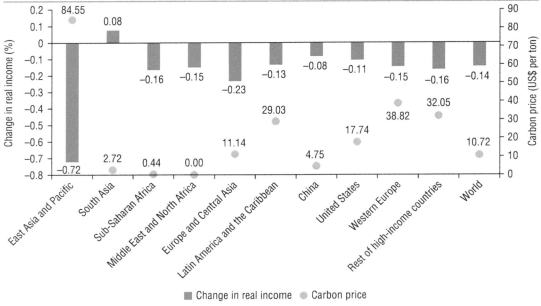

Sources: World Bank calculations; Chepeliev et al. 2021.
Note: The world's average carbon price is a weighted average carbon price.

The carbon prices that would be required to achieve NDC targets in a post-COVID world lead to moderately negative macroeconomic impacts, as per capita income reduction in most regions does not exceed 0.2 percent (figure 5.1). The only region with a larger reduction in income per capita is East Asia and Pacific (−0.72 percent), the result of its relatively ambitious emissions reduction target (24 percent relative to the 2030 baseline).

Table 5.1 shows the three sectors in each region with the largest reduction in output following the implementation of NDCs. As expected, the coal sector is the most affected sector in all regions. An increase in carbon prices under the NDC scenario leads to a reduction in global demand for coal, and the production of this commodity drops significantly in each region—ranging from between 6 percent and 7 percent in the Middle East and North Africa and China to between 20 percent and 30 percent in Europe, Latin America, the United States, and other high-income regions and countries. The gas sector (extraction and distribution) is the second-most-affected sector in almost half the regions analyzed. Given the increase in fuel prices following the implementation of carbon taxes, transportation (air, water, and ground transport) is likewise among the most affected sectors. All other sectors experience much less significant reductions in output.

Consistent with the observed changes in patterns of production, exports and imports of fossil fuels are affected the most. With lower global demand for fossil fuels, the volume of trade for these commodities declines, while trade is relocated modestly toward destinations with less stringent environmental regulations. For instance, China,

TABLE 5.1 Changes in Output Following the Implementation of Nationally Determined Contributions, by Sector and Region

Region	Most affected sector		Second-most affected sector		Third-most affected sector	
	Sector	Change (%)	Sector	Change (%)	Sector	Change (%)
China	Coal extraction	−6.0	Gas extraction and distribution	−3.0	Wearing apparel and leather products	−0.2
East Asia and Pacific	Air transport	−10.6	Coal extraction	−8.6	Other transport	−5.8
Europe	Coal extraction	−33.2	Air transport	−2.5	Gas extraction and distribution	−2.2
Europe and Central Asia	Coal extraction	−15.7	Gas extraction and distribution	−1.1	Nonmetallic minerals	−0.6
Latin America and Caribbean	Coal extraction	−18.3	Gas extraction and distribution	−3.3	Refined oil	−1.3
Middle East and North Africa	Coal extraction	−5.7	Gas extraction and distribution	−0.3	Wearing apparel and leather products	−0.2
Rest of high-income countries	Coal extraction	−18.5	Gas extraction and distribution	−3.3	Textiles	−1.2
South Asia	Coal extraction	−6.1	Wearing apparel and leather products	−0.4	Gas extraction and distribution	−0.4
Sub-Saharan Africa	Coal extraction	−8.9	Gas extraction and distribution	−0.2	Meat products (including fisheries) and other food	−0.2
United States	Coal extraction	−25.0	Gas extraction and distribution	−4.9	Other transport	−0.5
World	Coal extraction	−10.9	Gas extraction and distribution	−2.2	Air transport	−0.9

Sources: World Bank calculations; Chepeliev et al. 2021.
Note: The "other transport" sector refers to water and ground transport. For each region, the top three sectors with the largest reduction in output are shown. Percentage changes indicate the corresponding change in output in 2030 relative to the post-COVID baseline.

being the world's largest net importer of fossil fuels and having a relatively low carbon price consistent with its NDC target, experiences an increase in imports of fossil fuel commodities. Both East Asia and Sub-Saharan Africa, being large net energy exporters, experience a reduction in exports of fossil fuels. In the case of Sub-Saharan Africa, the reduction in fossil fuel exports is compensated for by an increase in exports of other goods and services, including agricultural commodities.

Implementation of the European Green Deal will likely have moderate negative impacts on the real per capita incomes of the EU's trading partners beyond those related to the NDCs. These impacts will be driven by two key factors. First, the significantly higher carbon price in the EU (from US$39 per ton of CO_2 under the NDC target to US$213 per ton of CO_2 under the European Green Deal target) will substantially reduce demand for fossil fuels within the EU. This reduction in demand will adversely affect the Middle East and North Africa and the Central Asia regions, including the Russian Federation, as the EU is a primary destination of their fossil fuel exports (figure 5.2). The higher price of carbon will make production of energy-intensive products more expensive in the EU, which will have a negative effect on exports of such products. Second, implementation of the CBAM will further reduce

FIGURE 5.2 Impacts of the European Green Deal and CBAM on GDP per Capita, by EU Trading Region, 2030

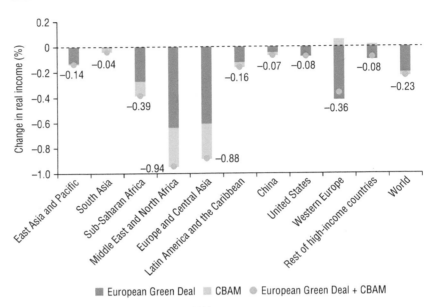

Sources: World Bank calculations; Chepeliev et al. 2021.
Note: CBAM = Carbon Border Adjustment Mechanism; EU = European Union. Figures represent % changes in 2030 relative to the baseline with implemented national determined contributions.

income in the EU's trading partners, not only the large energy exporters (Europe and Central Asia and Middle East and North Africa) but also China, a key exporter of energy-intensive chemical products to the EU. The EU carbon tax affects mainly the demand for and price of fossil fuels, while the CBAM affects more energy-intensive goods, such as metals, chemical products, nonmetallic minerals (cement, lime), and electricity. As a result, the main exporters of these commodities to the EU (Europe and Central Asia: chemicals, metals, and electricity; China and the Middle East and North Africa: chemicals) lie in regions that will experience negative consequences from implementation of the CBAM.

In this scenario, since the border tax is related to the carbon content of production in the exporting country, the impact of the CBAM across countries will be determined primarily by the carbon intensity of exports and the overall importance of exports to the EU (figure 5.3), noting that only commodities covered by the EU ETS sectors are subject to the tax.[12] The three regions most severely affected by the CBAM—Europe and Central Asia, Middle East and North Africa, and Sub-Saharan Africa—have both carbon-intensive exports and a relatively high share of EU-designated exports in GDP.

In terms of the changes in trade patterns, the European Green Deal primarily suppresses imports of fossil fuels and petroleum products because of lower EU-wide demand. Imports of coal will be affected the most, declining by 69 percent (table 5.2). This reduction in imports will result mainly from shrinking US exports. Imports of electricity, nonmetallic minerals, and wood and paper products will also see

FIGURE 5.3 Impacts of CBAM on Income per Capita and Carbon Intensity of Exports to the European Union, by EU Trading Region, 2030

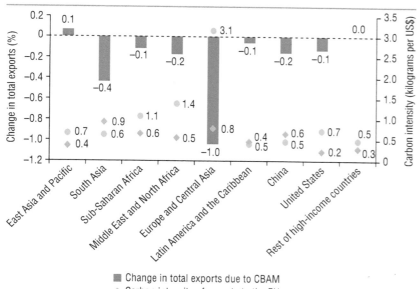

■ Change in total exports due to CBAM
◆ Carbon intensity of exports to the EU
● Share of exports to the EU in country's GDP

Sources: World Bank calculations; Chepeliev et al. 2021.
Note: CBAM = Carbon Border Adjustment Mechanism; EU = European Union. Figures represent % changes in 2030 relative to the European Green Deal implementation scenario.

TABLE 5.2 Impact of the European Green Deal and CBAM on Selected Sectors of EU Trading Partners

Percentage

Sector	Change in EU imports	Key source region	Share of total imports	Change in exports to EU for key source region	Change in total exports for key source region	Change in output for key source region
Coal	−69.1	United States	38.9	−70.8	−19.7	−5.4
Electricity	−28.2	Europe and Central Asia	58.2	−34.3	−15.6	−1.2
Nonmetallic minerals	−28.0	China	48.7	−33.8	−4.2	−0.2
Wood and paper products	−28.0	China	33.9	−37.5	−7.4	−0.6
Chemicals	−23.2	China	18.4	−38.4	−5.8	−0.7
Metals	−23.0	Europe and Central Asia	26.6	−38.7	−9.2	−3.2
Natural gas	−22.8	Europe and Central Asia	45.9	−20.9	−9.1	−1.5
Petroleum products	−11.5	Europe and Central Asia	47.1	−12.6	−5.4	−1.2
Crude oil	−9.3	Europe and Central Asia	52.5	−5.6	−1.6	−0.4

Sources: World Bank calculations; Chepeliev et al. 2021.
Note: CBAM = Carbon Border Adjustment Mechanism; EU = European Union. The share in total imports for key source regions is estimated for total imports, excluding intra-EU trade. For chemical products, the second-most-important EU trading partner (China) is presented; for the most important partner (the United States), observed changes in flows are insignificant. Selected sectors with the largest reduction in EU imports are presented.

significant declines. However, the reallocation of exports to other destinations and to the domestic market means that the fall in total exports (by product and region) will be much smaller than the reduction in exports to the EU and the impact on overall output will be small, except for coal and metals. Europe and Central Asia, together with China, are the country and regions with the largest number of sectors heavily engaged in trade with the EU that will be affected adversely by the European Green Deal and CBAM. These commodities include electricity, natural gas, oil, petroleum products, and metals for Europe and Central Asia and nonmetallic minerals, wood products, and chemicals for China.

While the CBAM will have a heavy impact on goods and services and whole production emits large amounts of carbon, new opportunities will arise in low-carbon activities. Opportunities may arise to attract energy-intensive products to countries that can provide low- or zero-carbon sources of energy, such as those that generate electricity without fossil fuels, including hydro, wind, and solar. Further, as trade in carbon-intensive products declines, suppliers in less carbon-intensive sectors—such as electronics, motor vehicles and parts, and other light manufacturing—will see increasing demand for their goods. Thus, climate mitigation policies not only lead to the decarbonization of the economy but also stimulate higher integration into the global value chains of non-carbon-intensive commodities. Countries that are already heavily involved in these global value chains or have the potential to participate in them will see new opportunities for trade.

Modeling the impacts of the CBAM is at a nascent stage but could inform discussions on the program that is being devised. Hence, it is important to explore the potential impacts, especially on low- and middle-income countries, of different modalities of design and implementation. Among these impacts are the source of information on the carbon content of products, the sector coverage, and the scope of carbon measurement. For example, if default values are used, how would allowing countries to demonstrate their carbon competitiveness relative to the benchmark affect the pattern of trade flows and the achievement of emissions targets?

Simulations from structural models also need to be complemented by detailed sector and country studies. It would be useful to assess the extent to which IO data accurately capture the realities and dynamics of carbon content for different products from different regions. For example, some countries are shifting quickly away from fossil fuels and to renewables, which may not be captured in current IO tables. For some of the poorest countries, available IO data are limited at best.

Private carbon management and integration of firms in low-income countries into global value chains

The public, as consumers and through nongovernmental organizations, is pushing global businesses to act on climate change. Measures adopted by the private sector can have major impacts on trade and the ability of small firms in low- and middle-income countries to remain or become global-value-chain suppliers. Carbon labeling was an early business response to consumer concerns; it measures the carbon footprint of a product from the production of raw materials and intermediate inputs through the value chain, ending with the consumption, disposal, or recycling of the product. The footprint is displayed on individual products, giving consumers the option of reducing or increasing their impact on the climate. Despite considerable interest and efforts by companies a decade or so ago,[13] many carbon-labeling initiatives have been discontinued or scaled down, reflecting major challenges with carbon labeling.

First, carbon labeling is methodologically complex, often expensive, and difficult for consumers to understand. Extensive data are needed for detailed carbon accounting. In principle, carbon footprinting requires measuring emissions at every point along every possible value chain and doing so frequently, as suppliers may switch their suppliers (each with its own carbon footprint) or adjust their production technology. The more detailed the calculations, the more expensive they will be. Presenting the information in a way that allows consumers to make meaningful decisions is also problematic.

Second, measurement is based on carbon-footprinting methodologies developed predominantly by industrial countries for use in industrial-country contexts (Brenton, Edwards-Jones, and Jensen 2009; Plassmann et al. 2010). The choice of methodology, limited data availability, and uncertainty about key variables can paint a misleading picture of the carbon footprint of exports from low- and middle-income countries. For example, a study of sugar exports from Malawi and Mauritius finds that if one of the main standards developed for carbon accounting—the Publicly Available Specification (PAS) 2050 developed by the British Standards Institute—were applied in the calculation, emissions associated with changes in land use would dominate the estimated carbon footprint. This reflects the fact that, in low- and middle-income countries, prior land use is often unknown; in that case, PAS 2050 prescribes the use of a worst-case benchmark—in the case of sugar, increasing the carbon calculation by 1,900 percent (Plassmann et al. 2010). When land-use change is not important, variables such as electricity emissions factors,[14] capital inputs, and loss of soil carbon have significant impacts on the carbon footprint. Therefore, it is important that the developers and users of standards apply emissions factors relevant for low- and middle-income countries and that there is transparency in the use of carbon-accounting methodologies and data sources and in how uncertainties and variability are addressed.

While the costs of carbon accounting, the methodological uncertainties, and the difficulties consumers have in using the displayed information led to a drop in the use of carbon labeling, calls for carbon-labeling programs have reappeared in recent years, along with a rise in concerns about climate change. Carbon labeling still looms as a strategy to engage involvement more actively in the fight against climate change, and its resurrection in a different form cannot be ruled out. In the past decade, research communities have developed better emissions data, which should allow the required calculations to be made at a lower cost. Different—easier to understand—ways of presenting the information to consumers could be developed, probably in the form of a traffic light system rather than mere numbers.

More and more private firms have pledged to reduce their carbon emissions and are engaging in some form of business carbon management, but without labeling individual products. Business carbon management has gone from aiming to provide information to, and influence the decisions of, consumers to being used for firms' management—which often has a team of experts at its disposal for collecting and processing carbon-accounting data. Today, more firms than ever before are calculating their carbon footprint; but rather than using those data to label individual products, they are using the information to identify areas in their value chains where emissions can be cut by reducing inputs like heat and electricity. Firms are monitoring their total emissions, assessing the impact of measures taken to reduce them, and publicizing their efforts as total firm savings, often through reports on the social and environmental impacts of their business activities. Carbon accounting allows firms to demonstrate how their activities are contributing to emissions reductions.

To appreciate the challenges facing large firms sourcing from global value chains, it is useful to understand the basics of carbon reporting. As discussed earlier, emissions are categorized in three groups: scope 1, scope 2, and scope 3. Scope 1 and scope 2 emissions are relatively easy for a firm to report (and easier to affect because they are under the firm's direct control). Scope 3 emissions are more challenging, both for reporting and achieving emissions reductions. The longer and more complex the value chain, the more difficult it is to identify and calculate scope 3 emissions.[15] The issues that Walmart faced with implementation of its Project Gigaton provide valuable insights in this context (box 5.3).

The experience of large firms such as Walmart and Unilever suggests that business carbon management programs need to address two important issues: first, gaining a better understanding of emissions along complex value chains and implementing appropriate solutions; and second, convincing the public that they are implementing credible measures to solve environmental problems. To address these challenges, firms have joined forces, sometimes with nongovernmental organizations, to pool resources and allow independent bodies to contribute to the design and implementation of

---

BOX 5.3 Implementation Challenges for Business Carbon Management: Walmart's Project Gigaton

For large and diversified companies such as Walmart, most carbon emissions are probably scope 3 emissions. These emissions originate not in Walmart's distribution centers and stores but during the production, transporting, and consumption of the many products destined for Walmart's shelves. Working with nongovernmental organizations, Walmart has identified six areas with the greatest opportunities for reducing emissions: energy use, sustainable agriculture, waste management, deforestation, packaging, and product use. Walmart reports that it has worked with the World Wildlife Fund on the overall concept and design of Project Gigaton and with other nongovernmental organizations—including the Environmental Defense Fund, Conservation International, the Nature Conservancy, the Sustainable Packaging Coalition, and the Carbon Disclosure Project[a]—to connect suppliers to measurement methodologies, guidance, and practical tools to help them to reduce emissions. Walmart has specified accounting methodologies for each area.[b]

Connecting with suppliers is key to the success of Project Gigaton in terms of emissions reduction. Suppliers set up an account within the project and report their progress each year according to established measurement methodologies. They then receive guidance from Walmart and its partners. More than 1,000 suppliers have signed on to Project Gigaton; in the first two years of the project, they have reported a total reduction of 94 million tons of CO_2 emissions.

Walmart reports that, while it plans to enlarge the scope of areas for reduction, it faces difficulties. Nearly 80 percent of reported reductions are in energy use, while progress on deforestation and sustainable agriculture requires "influencing a disparate set of actors far upstream in the supply chain, addressing interdependencies and barriers in complex social and economic systems, and gaining alignment with others regarding methodologies for measurement and action." Walmart is working with suppliers and nongovernmental organizations to support the development of tools to enable some improvement in these areas. In its environmental reports, Walmart does not identify the extent to which it is seeking to reduce emissions in its global supply chains compared to its US sources.

a. A not-for-profit organization that runs a leading global disclosure system.

b. For information on Walmart's Project Gigaton, see https://www.walmartsustainabilityhub.com/climate/project-gigaton.

instruments, hoping to convince the public of the sincerity of their efforts.[16] Multistakeholder initiatives are voluntary in nature (as opposed to government-enforced regulation) but may establish de facto mandatory market requirements because of the influence of large retailers or brands. Thus, when such initiatives adopt standards and codes, these standards often end up dominating certain market segments, and suppliers in low- and middle-income countries may only gain access to these segments by complying with the requirements of the initiative.[17]

The difference between carbon-labeling initiatives and business carbon management is the scope of the initiatives and how the results of carbon accounting are used. Carbon labeling requires all carbon emissions to be analyzed and results to be displayed on individual products. Business carbon management rarely includes a full overview of a firm's carbon emissions but instead focuses on selected segments for which the firm sets emissions targets. The analytical results are used to verify progress in complying with reduction targets and are communicated through corporate materials. Both approaches rely on globally accepted measurement standards and methodologies. Walmart's supply chain work, for instance, is based on identifying hotspots, especially for energy use, and on reducing hotspot emissions, rather than on determining the carbon footprint of products. Carbon accounting is used as a research tool to identify where savings can be made.

How firms in industrial countries endeavor to reduce scope 3 emissions may determine future market access for low-income and other countries. There is very little empirical evidence on the consequences of industrial-country firms, such as retailers and big global brands, putting pressure on their suppliers to reduce carbon emissions. But it is very likely that the resulting impact on suppliers, including low-income-country producers, will be significant. The ability to reduce carbon emissions in a verifiable way may become a major source of competitiveness in market segments catering to climate-conscious buyers.[18]

The standards and methodologies used for carbon footprinting in these business carbon management initiatives have been developed primarily by actors from industrial countries working for firms in these countries.[19] Even development of the scope 3 standard has been influenced heavily by industrial countries, despite the fact that value chains often reach into low- and middle-income countries and the cheapest options for reducing carbon emissions could be found in their segments of these chains.

Complex value chains in low- and middle-income countries, especially in low-income countries, often lack traceability and relevant data. Some industrial-country firms involved in these value chains have recognized this issue and have joined initiatives to incentivize other firms in these value chains to reduce their emissions. For example, the Value Change Program seeks to allow firms to get credit for emissions reductions, even if poor traceability and conventional methods of carbon footprinting make it impossible to determine the exact volume of emissions reductions associated with the products being purchased through the value chain (Gold Standard 2018; SBTi, Navigant, and Gold Standard 2018).[20]

Business carbon management was not developed with a development perspective. Documents describing methodologies refer only to development issues in generic terms. Key issues, such as land-use change and carbon sequestration, can be critical sources of emissions reduction, but current standards do not allow companies to get credit for savings in these areas. Recognizing the development dimension should be a fundamental part of understanding the nature of business operations in low-income countries and thus in making the right business and climate change mitigation decisions.

Hence, the challenge is how to ensure that poor countries' interests are reflected in the development of carbon-accounting standards and methodologies and that the realities of their conditions are reflected in the databases used in emissions reduction initiatives.

There is a general lack of knowledge of how low-income-country value chains perform in terms of carbon emissions and how poor countries will fit into future value chains under business carbon management. Low-income countries need to understand their "carbon competitiveness" in key exports, including the pattern of their emissions compared with those of other countries, and the ability of their producers to benefit from "carbon efficiencies," through instruments such as sustainability criteria, standards, and certification. Further research on this emerging policy issue is required. This effort needs to be combined with the much richer literature on standards and low-income-country exports to address the question of how climate-friendly global value chains can also be turned into inclusive global value chains.

Greening transport: Implications for low-income-country exports

Climate change mitigation includes a series of measures that are likely to increase the transport costs of traded goods, including the exports of low- and middle-income countries. There is a popular perception that the emissions from international transport are a hotspot in supply chains and that they should be reduced as much as possible. To this end, exports from countries that use carbon-intensive transport modes and are located far from global markets could be penalized—for example, by limiting the transporting of fresh produce exports to market by air or tourism in remote low-income countries. Two key questions arise in this context: (1) Will low- and middle-income countries be able to exploit new, more carbon-efficient transport modes? and (2) If, and how, will low-income countries be exempted from policy measures that affect the transporting of traded goods? On the plus side, mitigation may also open new export markets, exemplified by the opportunity for low- and middle-income countries to start producing and supplying zero-emission fuels (Englert and Losos 2020).

This section briefly reviews the evidence on how transportation costs affect the volume and structure of exports and how mitigation measures might affect costs. It also looks at the export structure of low-income countries and how emissions are distributed in the global supply chains of which low-income countries are a part. This discussion should lead to a better understanding of how vulnerable poor countries are to increased transport costs caused by mitigation. While the discussion focuses on air and sea transport, several low- and middle-income countries are investing heavily in rail transport, which can be both more cost-effective and less emissive than road transport.

Sea transport costs may be affected by mitigation measures. Both the International Maritime Organization (IMO) and individual firms have been active in developing mitigation measures. In April 2018, the IMO committed to reducing the 2008 levels of emissions in the shipping sector by 50 percent by 2050. Some firms have set higher targets: the world's biggest container shipper, Maersk, aims to be carbon-neutral by 2050. Shipping companies also work collectively outside of the IMO. Maersk has pledged to work with industry players like ABS, Cargill, MAN, Mitsubishi, and Siemens to establish a research center of 100 scientists to support a reduction in carbon emissions from shipping.

Policy makers are considering instruments to incentivize the shipping industry to adopt low-carbon forms of sea transport. The Paris Agreement did not include specific language on shipping and air travel. Some observers argue that this omission is explained by the fact that the two relevant United Nations agencies, the International Civil Aviation Organization (ICAO) and the IMO, are working with countries to mitigate the emissions associated with international transport. Of course, individual countries may still include targets for these two international activities in their national mitigation plans and might be able to act more effectively than the two United Nations agencies. The EU, for example, has proposed to include shipping in the EU ETS if talks with the IMO to reduce emissions fail. This inclusion would put a price on emissions from shipping.

Aviation, for both freight and passengers, is also under pressure to reduce emissions, as illustrated by the "flight shame" consumer phenomenon and no-fly campaigns. The ICAO has adopted a mitigation policy based on technological improvements, including setting emissions standards and introducing biofuels, supporting operational improvements through fuel efficiency monitoring and more direct flight paths, making airports more fuel-efficient, and capping CO_2 emissions at their 2019 level[21] and offsetting aviation's CO_2 emissions[22] above this level through the Carbon Offsetting and Reduction Scheme for International Aviation (CORSIA). CORSIA is the centerpiece of the aviation response, at least in the short run, as—contrary to shipping—new technologies that may mitigate aviation's contribution to global warming are far from fully developed.

Airlines from 80 countries, representing 77 percent of international air traffic, have joined CORSIA's voluntary first phase (2021–26). Joining will become mandatory in 2027 for states with large aviation industries. The United States has joined the program, while China has not. Routes that depart from or land in poor, small island, and landlocked low- and middle-income countries are exempt from the offsetting requirement. CORSIA also exempts countries with very small aviation industries, very small operators, and very small planes, as well as flights for medical emergencies, disaster response, and other humanitarian purposes. Furthermore, CORSIA only covers civil aviation; presidential, police, customs, and military flights are excluded. Given these and other exceptions, CORSIA will only cover about 40 percent of global aviation (Hedley and Rock 2016).

National efforts may be more important than the ICAO policy. The EU and European Economic Area formally included the aviation industry in its ETS as of January 2012. Initially, all flights from and to EU airports were included, except for those of low-income countries. The inclusion of out-of-EU flights, however, gave rise to strong protests from the EU's trading partners, like China and the United States, and subsequently, the EU included only intra-EU flights. The EC has argued that it reduced the scope of its aviation policy to give the ICAO time to agree on a global measure. The exemption of flights out of Europe has been extended to 2024, after which the EU may decide to include all flights if it is not satisfied with the level of ambition and operation of CORSIA.

The costs of the emerging mitigation measures in international transport are not easy to assess, as the policy and business instruments are still under discussion, new technologies are still under development, and COVID-19 has (at least temporarily) changed travel habits. What is clear, however, is that the cost implications will be more manageable in shipping than in aviation. Shipping already is a relatively carbon-efficient way to move goods and can be made less emissive in many ways—by lowering vessel speed and developing carbon-neutral fuels, among others. In aviation, potential carbon-efficient technologies are harder to develop. Mitigation measures in shipping are likely to increase the import price of goods only marginally. For example, certain measures that raise the costs of bunker fuel by between US$10 and US$50 per ton of CO_2 equivalent may increase maritime transport costs by between 0.4 percent and 16 percent. Yet this cost increase will, in turn, raise the price of imported goods by less than 1 percent (Halim, Smith, and Englert 2019).

The share of international transport in a good's carbon footprint is often small. Costa Rican coffee exemplifies the minor share of transport in commodity exports, as shown in table 5.3. Farm-level emissions are significant (20 percent), caused mainly by fertilizers (19 percent), but consumers are responsible for nearly half of the total. International transport accounts for only 4 percent of total emissions along the value chain. Changing consumer behavior is more likely to have a large impact on the carbon footprint of a commodity like coffee than reducing emissions from shipping.

The impact of mitigation measures on aviation may be larger than the impact on shipping. While CORSIA will exempt low-income countries, it will affect a range of neighboring low-income countries. Some countries are participating voluntarily.[23] South Africa is expected to join once CORSIA becomes mandatory (2027), as may other larger African countries, given that their aviation sector exceeds the threshold. Low-income-country freight and passenger travel may be affected if it is routed through participating countries.

The proposed mitigation measures do, however, appear to be modest. The EU ETS may include international aviation, implying higher costs than CORSIA. Today, the EU ETS's impact, even on flights that are included, is minimal because of the free

TABLE 5.3 Carbon Footprint of 1 Kilogram of Green Coffee

Stage	Amount (kilogram of CO_2 equivalent)	Share (%)
In Costa Rica	1.50	31
Farm	1.02	20
Fertilizers	0.96	19
Mill	0.48	10
Exportation	0.27	6
International shipping[a]	0.19	4
In Europe	3.05	63
Roasting	0.19	4
Packaging	0.13	3
Distribution	0.15	3
Grinding and purchasing	0.29	6
Consumption	2.15	45
Disposal	0.14	3
Total	**4.82**	**100**

Source: Killian et al. 2013.
a. From Costa Rica to Europe.

allocation of many permits and the generally low price of the permits that are sold. Transport & Environment, an environmental nongovernmental organization, has calculated that the extra costs of an economy ticket on an Oslo-Rome flight would be less than €4 (US$4.50) per return ticket. When the EU first discussed including aviation in its ETS, the EC expected only modest increases for tickets to a typical tourist destination. Good (2010) estimates that the program, as initially proposed, would have increased the cost of a return ticket to the Caribbean by €16 to €20. The impact on tourism, including in low-income countries, is particularly difficult to assess because it depends on the EU's practice of distributing many allowances for free and on the volatile market price for allowances that are sold. Nevertheless, low- and middle-income countries that rely heavily on price-sensitive tourism may be strongly affected if such programs are tightened by raising the price of the allowances sold.

The carbon footprint of air transport of goods may be small relative to emissions at other points along the value chain. Studies of the horticulture sector have shown that imports by air from, typically, low-income countries that use sunshine, manual labor, and natural compost in production generate fewer emissions than producers in nearby countries that use heated greenhouses, tractors, and fertilizers. Again, emissions at the consumption stage often dominate. Based on these studies, during a debate on so-called food miles and aviation hotspots, a UK minister of trade noted, "Driving 6.5 miles to buy your shopping emits more carbon than flying a pack of Kenyan green beans to the United Kingdom" (IATA 2012).

Other aspects of trade supply chains also offer significant opportunities for reducing carbon emissions and for increasing the use of measurement and monitoring to guide interventions. For example, delays at borders and ports can be a major source of emissions. Delays at the California–Baja California land border crossings reportedly result in an average of 457 tons of CO_2 equivalent emissions each day, equivalent to the consumption of more than 51,400 gallons of gasoline (NBC San Diego 2021). Delays at borders and ports are prevalent in low- and middle-income countries and offer the opportunity for interventions that not only reduce carbon emissions but also increase economic efficiency. Investments in port equipment, the streamlining and automation of customs clearance and immigration procedures, and policy reforms that increase the transparency and predictability of policies applied at the border are central to curbing delays. These measures could be complemented by reforms that support the modernization of trucking fleets and investments in green logistics.

Delays and inefficiencies in the international transport of goods also affect carbon emissions indirectly. The Food and Agriculture Organization estimates that about 1.3 billion tons of food, approximately 30 percent of global production, is lost each year. Food production is also a major source of carbon emissions, and reducing food waste would substantially reduce emissions. In the process of trading food, inefficient logistics and border and port *delays* account for a significant amount of wasted food.[24] This waste is compounded by poor border and logistics *infrastructure* that provides little protection from high temperatures and rain for food products kept in storage or held at the border for inspection. Hence, facilitating the trade of agricultural products, improving transport and logistics procedures and infrastructure for food trade in low- and middle-income countries, and reducing nontariff barriers related to sanitary and phytosanitary requirements could have multiple benefits. These benefits include improving efficiency in agriculture and transportation, boosting trade in food products, increasing returns to farmers, lowering prices for consumers, and reducing carbon emissions from agriculture.

Conclusions

Measures to reduce carbon emissions are becoming more and more important. As these measures will affect the trade of low- and middle-income countries the most, their interests should be well understood and taken into account in the design of such measures. This challenge is palpable in the discussions of the CBAM—in terms of the methods and data used to calculate the carbon content of products, the boundaries for the calculation, the use of benchmarks, the range of products covered, and so on. A key issue in this context is whether individual countries will be allowed to demonstrate their carbon competitiveness relative to the defined benchmarks.

Initial simulations of the potential economywide impacts of the EU's CBAM suggest that, if the number of sectors covered is limited to those that are most emissive, fossil fuel exporters and countries producing the most energy-intensive products (such as steel) will bear the brunt of the program. Yet even for the steel sector, the impact on producers in low- and middle-income countries could vary considerably, depending on the details of the final program. Despite the negative implications for these countries, carbon reduction requirements may be tightened—by increasing the number of sectors covered and widening the scope of the CBAM—to keep the 1.5°C global warming target within reach. Hence, it is paramount to understand how low- and middle-income countries, and their trade, will be affected by the standards and approaches being considered in the design of this program. In general, it will be important to ensure that these designs are not focused too narrowly.

In addition to government measures to reduce carbon emissions, private programs are being developed and implemented that will have an impact on low-income-country trade, perhaps to a greater extent than government policies. Again, considering the interests of low- and middle-income countries in the design and implementation of such programs is essential to ensure that they do not hinder the participation of carbon-competitive firms in these countries. This effort will require increasing the capacity of low- and middle-income countries to identify and understand the areas in which they are carbon competitive; implementing measures that help firms to reduce their emissions (for example, giving access to new, low-carbon technologies through trade); and investing in traceability and testing and certification systems so that firms can verify their conformity with the carbon-related requirements of buyers in overseas markets. These areas are where institutions such as the World Bank and the WTO can step in—offering technical assistance and capacity-building resources, especially to low-income countries.

Trade-related transport is another area being explored for greenhouse gas mitigation opportunities. While air transport is a hotspot, it is not necessarily the subsector with the largest potential for reducing carbon emissions along a trade supply chain. However, emissions can definitely be reduced—in combination with higher efficiency in trading—by curbing delays at borders and along value chains. This area is particularly relevant for perishable products, as delays lead to food waste.

Notes

1. An emissions trading system or program, also known as a cap-and-trade system, sets a desired maximum ceiling (or cap) for emissions and lets the market determine the price for keeping emissions below that cap. To comply with their emissions targets at the lowest possible cost, regulated entities can undertake internal abatement measures, acquire allowances, or reduce their emissions, depending on the relative costs of these options (PMR 2017, 160).

2. The mechanism of carbon leakage sketched here is the *competitiveness* mechanism. Other mechanisms exist, including one that works through the *price of fossil-based fuel*. Lowering the demand for fuel in regulated countries will lower fuel prices, which will, in turn, raise demand in unregulated countries, thus canceling parts of the carbon savings realized in countries that have introduced carbon regulation. Another mechanism works through *capital markets,* where capital seeks unregulated markets that offer opportunities to make higher profits. These alternative carbon leakage mechanisms are not considered here because this report focuses on the potential impacts of one particular mitigation instrument—border adjustments—and not on carbon leakage per se. Border adjustment measures address carbon leakage through the competitiveness mechanism. Arroyo-Currás et al. (2015) analyze different mechanisms of carbon leakage in global energy markets.

3. Carbon border adjustments are taxes on imports and rebates on exports that account for variance in carbon-pricing policies across different countries.

4. Many economists strongly support carbon border adjustments, considering them to be an appropriate instrument for correcting the market failure of too low prices on carbon emissions. In that way, using border adjustments becomes a textbook example of correcting an externality by applying a Pigouvian tax. A statement of support for carbon taxes, including carbon border adjustment, published in the *Wall Street Journal* on January 17, 2019, by a large and bipartisan (in the US political context) group of economists—including 27 Nobel laureates—exemplifies economists' support (*Economist* 2019).

5. If a carbon tax based on the carbon footprint is deemed an indirect tax (that is, similar to a value added tax), there would be no violation of GATT principles in Article III:2, provided the tax levied on imported products is equivalent to the tax imposed on domestic products, based on their carbon footprint. But there are two challenges in this context. First, taxing some of the carbon emissions from the life cycle carbon footprint of a product (for example, emissions from some production processes) could be considered a direct tax. GATT rules generally do not allow direct taxes to be adjusted at the border (that is, charged on imports or exempted for exports). Second, the carbon cost measure—such as an emissions trading program—could be viewed not as a tax but rather as a regulation (thus falling under the purview of GATT Article III:4). In both cases, the adjustment to imports could be incompatible with substantive GATT disciplines, although GATT Article XX could theoretically be invoked to justify it, as long as the carbon footprint of imported and domestic products is accounted for correctly, the border adjustment is appropriate, and the program respects relevant rules to ensure that the climate objective is pursued coherently.

6. Life cycle analysis is a method used to evaluate the environmental impact of a product throughout its life cycle—encompassing extraction and processing of raw materials, manufacturing, distribution, use, recycling, and final disposal.

7. The US Congress has discussed a carbon border adjustment program many times. These discussions have been linked to bills on taxing carbon introduced in the Senate, the House of Representatives, or both. These bills propose to levy taxes or implement a cap-and-trade system.

8. The proposal requires taking into account the embedded emissions in material inputs used in the production process. For imported inputs, it is not clear how the calculation will take into account carbon policies in the country of production. The calculation and verification process could be quite complex.

9. The EU proposal further allows default values to be adapted if specific data on objective factors—such as geography, natural resources, market conditions, energy mix, or industrial production—are available.

10. See ECRST (2021), which studies the economic impact that the EU's CBAM could potentially have on foreign exporters of products to the EU market.

11. It should be noted that these simulations were performed prior to the July 2021 announcement of the specifics in the EU's Carbon Border Adjustment Mechanism.

12. This list is somewhat broader than the list of commodities covered in the initial CBAM proposal of the EU.

13. The UK supermarket Tesco was a frontrunner in carbon labeling. In 2007 its chief executive promised a revolution in green consumption and pledged to label Tesco's 50,000 own-brand products with the total amount of carbon emissions from production to consumption. Carbon labeling spread quickly, and numerous retailers and brands, especially in Northern Europe and the United States, began counting carbon and displaying their calculations on their products. In 2012, however, Tesco gave up. By then, it had labeled only about 500 products (Lucas and Clark 2012).

14. An *emissions factor* converts activity data into greenhouse gas emissions data—for example, kilograms of CO_2 equivalent emitted per liter of fuel consumed or kilograms of CO_2 equivalent emitted per kilometer traveled (PMR 2017).

15. As an example, Unilever, a producer of consumer products, reports that emissions from its own factories amount to less than 5 percent of the total carbon footprint of its products. Consumer use accounts for more than 60 percent of its carbon footprint, and raw materials account for about 25 percent. See https://www.unilever.com/sustainable-living/reducing-environmental-impact/greenhouse-gases/Our-greenhouse-gas-footprint.

16. Such joint efforts are known as "multistakeholder initiatives," "collective governance," and "sustainability roundtables." Some examples include the Forest Stewardship Council, the Marine Stewardship Council, the Roundtable on Sustainable Palm Oil, the Roundtable on Responsible Soy, the Roundtable on the Better Cotton Initiative, the Rainforest Alliance, and the Extractive Industries Transparency Initiative. Sometimes such multistakeholder initiatives involve public sector bodies and international agencies.

17. Businesses often join initiatives led by nongovernmental organizations to be able to tap more resources and commit to emissions reductions in a credible way by using internationally accepted measurement standards and methodologies and allowing independent bodies to verify their reductions. The Science Based Target initiative (SBTi) is one such initiative; it assists firms in setting and verifying carbon reduction targets. The targets may be set at different levels of ambition and scope, depending on the nature and capacities of the participating firms. When scope 3 emissions cover more than 40 percent of total emissions, firms are required to include an "ambitious and measurable" scope 3 target. The clothing brand H&M, for example, aims to be "climate-positive" in its entire supply chain (reducing emissions by more than its value chains emit) by 2040, to reduce scope 1 and 2 emissions by 40 percent by 2030, and to reduce scope 3 emissions from purchased raw materials, fabric production, and garments by 59 percent by 2030. H&M has committed to these targets through the SBTi.

18. The SBTi views the setting of reduction targets for scope 3 emissions as a best practice and recommends that firms set scope 3 targets by screening their emissions along their value chains to gain insight into emissions hotspots and then focus on reducing emissions from these hotspots rather than from the whole value chain. More than 2,800 firms reported measurements of scope 3 emissions to the Carbon Disclosure Project in 2017. Of the firms measuring scope 3 emissions, 368 firms had set scope 3 emissions reduction targets.

19. The SBTi relies on the standards and methodologies of the Greenhouse Gas Protocol, a nongovernmental organization established by the World Resources Institute and the World Business Council for Sustainable Development. The Greenhouse Gas Protocol has produced one of the three dominant global standards for product-level carbon footprinting. The other two are the PAS 2050 and ISO 14067:2018. All three standards are based on the principles of life cycle analysis, as expressed in the ISO 14040 and ISO 14044 global

standards. The Greenhouse Gas Protocol has also produced a standard for scope 3 emissions accounting (Greenhouse Gas Protocol 2011) and a free, web-based tool—Scope 3 Evaluator—that allows users to make an initial, rough approximation of their full scope 3 footprint, regardless of the size or type of organization (https://ghgprotocol.org/scope-3-evaluator).

20. Danone provides a case study of the application of the Value Change approach. Danone's supply chain is complex and global. For example, milk is sourced directly from more than 100,000 suppliers, many of whom are small farmers. The company developed a framework of representative farms across the globe that are monitored daily and extrapolates data from these farms to similar ones to estimate emissions from its global activity. The data are analyzed to identify which farming practices drive the most improvement in soil carbon sequestration. The issue of soil carbon sequestration is a hot topic in the carbon-footprinting environment. Danone would like to get credit for savings in soil sequestration, but this is not possible under current standards, including those of the Greenhouse Gas Protocol (Plassmann and Norton 2017).

21. Originally, the baseline for emissions reductions was to be the average of emissions over 2019 and 2020. However, with COVID-19 drastically reducing air traffic and emissions in 2020, the impact on the CORSIA baseline would have been substantial. Recognizing this, the ICAO Council decided to use the value of 2019 emissions to avoid placing a higher economic burden on the aviation industry (ICAO 2020).

22. Airlines will only offset CO_2 emissions above their 2019 level; they will not address any other global warming impacts of aviation, such as emissions of nitrogen oxide and water vapor. There is considerable uncertainty about the importance of these other impacts, yet many observers believe that the global warming impact of aviation is twice the impact of its CO_2 emissions alone.

23. According to Kusova and Dufour (2019), the following African countries intend to participate: Burkina Faso, Cameroon, the Democratic Republic of Congo, Equatorial Guinea, Gabon, Ghana, Kenya, Namibia, Nigeria, Uganda, and Zambia.

24. An official UK estimate suggests that additional paperwork leading to border delays because of Brexit could result in 142,000 tons of food being wasted in the first six months of 2021 (Stone 2021).

References

Arroyo-Currás Tabaré, Nico Bauer, Elmar Kriegler, Valeria Jana Schwanitz, Gunnar Luderer, Tino Aboumahboub, Anastasis Giannousakis, and Jérôme Hilaire. 2015. "Carbon Leakage in a Fragmented Climate Regime: The Dynamic Response of Global Energy Markets." *Technological Forecasting and Social Change* 90 (A): 192–203. https://doi.org/10.1016/j.techfore.2013.10.002.

Brenton, Paul, Gareth Edwards-Jones, and Michael Friis Jensen. 2009. "Carbon Labeling and Low-Income Country Exports: A Review of the Development Issues." *Development Policy Review* 27 (3): 243–67.

Brenton, Paul, Gareth Edwards-Jones, and Michael Friis Jensen. 2010. *Carbon Footprints and Food Systems: Do Current Accounting Methodologies Disadvantage Developing Countries?* World Bank Study. Washington, DC: World Bank. https://openknowledge.worldbank.org/handle/10986/2506.

Chepeliev, Maksym, Maryla Maliszewska, Israel Osorio-Rodarte, Maria Filipa Seara e Pereira, and Dominique van der Mensbrugghe. 2021. "Pandemics, Climate Mitigation, and Re-Shoring: Impacts of a Changing Global Economy on Trade, Incomes, and Poverty." Policy Research Working Paper, World Bank, Washington, DC, forthcoming.

EC (European Commission). 2019. "The European Green Deal." Communication from the EC to the European Parliament, the European Council, the Council, the European Economic and Social Committee, and the Committee of the Regions, EC, Brussels. https://ec.europa .eu/info/sites/info/files/european-green-deal-communication_en.pdf.

EC (European Commission). 2021. "Proposal for a Regulation of the European Parliament and of the Council Establishing a Carbon Border Adjustment Mechanism." EC, Brussels. https:// ec.europa.eu/info/sites/default/files/carbon_border_adjustment_mechanism_0.pdf.

Economist. 2019. "Climate Change Targets: Omissions." *The Economist*, October 19. https:// www.economist.com/weeklyedition/2019-10-19.

Englert, Dominik, and Andrew Losos. 2020. "Zero-Emission Shipping: What's in It for Developing Countries?" *Transport for Development* (blog), February 24. https://blogs .worldbank.org/transport/zero-emission-shipping-whats-it-developing-countries.

ERCST (European Roundtable on Climate Change and Sustainable Transition). 2021. "Study on the Economic Impact That EU CBAM Could Potentially Impose on Foreign Exporters of Products to the EU Market." Draft report, ERCST, Brussels, February.

Gold Standard. 2018. "Value (Scope 3) Interventions—Greenhouse Gas Accounting and Reporting Guidance." Draft V6 for testing, September. Gold Standard Foundation, Geneva. https://www.goldstandard.org/sites/default/files/documents/2018_09_scope_3_guidance _testing_draft_v1pdf.pdf.

Good, Philip. 2010. "Tourism, Aviation and Emissions Trading." Caribbean Tourism Summit, Brussels, March 14. http://www.onecaribbean.org/content/files/Philip-Good-European -commission.pdf.

Greenhouse Gas Protocol. 2011. "Corporate Value Chain (Scope 3) Accounting and Reporting Standard." Greenhouse Gas Protocol, Washington, DC. https://ghgprotocol.org/standards /scope-3-standard.

Halim, Ronald A., Tristan Smith, and Dominik Englert. 2019. "Understanding the Economic Impacts of Greenhouse Gas Mitigation Policies on Shipping: What Is the State of the Art of Current Modeling Approaches?" Policy Research Working Paper 8695, World Bank, Washington, DC. https://ssrn.com/abstract=3320893.

Hedley, Adam, and Nicholas Rock. 2016. "First Ever Global Regime for Aviation Emissions: ICAO Adopts Global Market-Based Measure to Combat Aircraft CO_2 Emissions." Reed Smith Client Alerts, October 10. https://www.reedsmith.com/en/perspectives/2016/10 /first-ever-global-regime-for-aviation-emissions-ic.

IATA (International Air Transport Association). 2012. "Cargo's Carbon Emissions." *Airlines*, August 1. https://airlines.iata.org/analysis/cargos-carbon-emissions.

ICAO (International Civil Aviation Organization). 2020. "ICAO Council Agrees to the Safeguard Adjustment for CORSIA in Light of COVID-19 Pandemic." ICAO, Montreal, June 30. https:// www.icao.int/Newsroom/Pages/ICAO-Council-agrees-to-the-safeguard-adjustment-for -CORSIA-in-light-of-COVID19-pandemic.aspx.

Killian, Bernard, Lloyd Rivera, Melissa Soto, and David Navichoc. 2013. "Carbon Footprint across the Coffee Supply Chain: The Case of Costa Rican Coffee." *Journal of Agricultural Science and Technology B* 3 (3): 151–70.

Kusova, Beata, and Julien Dufour. 2019. "The CORSIA Reporting and Verification Season Will Start Soon! ICAO's CORSIA Update." *ICAO's CORSIA Newsletter,* December. https:// www.verifavia.com/gestion_newsletter/view_mailing.php?contact_id=71454&envoi _id=324&newsletter_id=551&clef=E6Vgk7RIaIYB.

Lucas, Louise, and Pilita Clark. 2012. "Tesco Steps Back on Carbon Footprint Labelling." *Financial Times*, January 31. https://www.ft.com/content/96fd9478-4b71-11e1-a325 -00144feabdc0.

Messerlin, Patrick A. 2012. "Climate and Trade Policies: From Mutual Destruction to Mutual Support." *World Trade Review* 11 (1): 53–80. doi:10.1017/S1474745611000395.

NBC San Diego. 2021. "Delays at Border Crossings Cost San Diego–Tijuana Region Billions: SANDAG Study." NBC San Diego, February 27. https://www.nbcsandiego.com/news

/local/delays-at-border-crossings-cost-san-diego-tijuana-region-billions-sandag-study/2533918/.

Plassmann, Katharina, and Andrew Norton. 2017. "Recognizing the Benefits of Above-Ground Carbon Sequestration in the Carbon Footprint of Products Derived from Woody Perennial Systems." *Carbon Management* 8 (4): 343–49. doi: 10.1080/17583004.2017.1362947.

Plassmann, Katharina, Andrew Norton, N. Attarzadeh, M. P. Jensen, P. Brenton, and G. Edwards-Jones. 2010. "Methodological Complexities of Product Carbon Footprinting: A Sensitivity Analysis of Key Variables in a Developing Country Context." *Environmental Science & Policy* 13 (5): 393–404. https://doi.org/10.1016/j.envsci.2010.03.013.PMR 2017

PMR (Partnership for Market Readiness). 2017. *Carbon Tax Guide: A Handbook for Policy Makers.* Washington, DC: World Bank.

SBTi (Science Based Targets initiative), Navigant, and Gold Standard. 2018a. "Value Change in the Value Chain: Best Practices in Scope 3 Greenhouse Gas Management. Version 3.0, November, Gold Standard Foundation, Geneva. https://sciencebasedtargets.org/resources/legacy/2018/12/SBT_Value_Chain_Report-1.pdf.

Stone, Jon. 2021. "Brexit Border Delays Could See 142,000 Tonnes of Food Wasted in Six Months, Government Estimates." *Independent,* January 29. https://www.independent.co.uk/news/uk/politics/brexit-border-food-waste-fish-seafood-meat-b1794364.html.

6

Issues at the Country Level:
A Diagnostic Framework

For all countries, access to no- or low-carbon technologies (through trade and foreign direct investment) will be critical to new growth strategies. The climate and trade policy diagnostic framework presented in appendix C is a tool for gathering information on the link between trade and climate at the country level. It is intended to help researchers and policy makers to identify (1) key vulnerabilities in trade to rising temperatures, changing precipitation, and greater frequency of extreme weather events; (2) areas where trade can play a key role in supporting mitigation and adaptation to a changing climate as well as emerging constraints; (3) regulatory gaps in the climate and trade policy environment; and (4) recommendations of climate-relevant trade policy options. This chapter provides country-specific highlights for Vietnam and Ethiopia.

Vietnam

Vietnam is vulnerable to tropical cyclones and storm surges, droughts, and floods and is considered one of the most hazard-prone countries in the world, with more than 80 storm events, around 45 million people affected, and nearly 19,000 killed from 1953 to 2010. Flooding is the second most threatening natural hazard, with around 60 major events, 5,000 killed, and 25 million affected in the past half century (World Bank and ADB 2020). Given its high exposure to floods and storms and the fact that two of its most important economic sectors—industry and agriculture—are located in coastal lowlands and deltas, Vietnam is one of the five countries that will be affected the most adversely by climate change. The United Nations Office for Disaster Risk Reduction (UNISDR) estimates Vietnam's average annual losses to disaster at around US$2.4 billion, or almost 1.5 percent of gross domestic product (GDP). The absolute value of losses is projected to rise dramatically over the coming years, as the value of both the exposed assets and the climate-related hazard rises (World Bank and ADB 2020).

Climate change will affect Vietnam's current and future trade flows, so favorable climate-relevant trade policies are necessary. Climate change will drive up the costs of production (through, for example, the destruction of trade-relevant infrastructure and the rising costs of raw materials, especially agricultural ones), and reduce the competitiveness of Vietnamese goods and services. Given the country's high level of trade openness and high ratio of trade to GDP, the rising costs of production will have a severe impact on welfare, productivity, trade performance, and balance of payments.

The nexus between climate change and trade is particularly relevant for Vietnam, for the following reasons:

- *Climate change poses significant risks to Vietnam's export trade performance, terms of trade, and balance of payments.* In addition to being an export-oriented economy with high trade openness, Vietnam is also an agricultural economy, with the majority of its populace employed in the sector, most of whom are smallholders (IFAD 2019, 4). Climate change will reshuffle the world's exporters and importers of agricultural products, altering comparative advantages in production and international trade by introducing new producers from high-income countries into a market that was limited to producers from low- and middle-income countries before significant climate changes had occurred (UNCTAD 2021, 12). In the rice market, traditional exporters—such as India, Pakistan, Thailand, the United States, and Vietnam—are projected to suffer large reductions in their rice yields and exports. Rice production will move north as new exporters emerge—namely, China, Japan, and the Republic of Korea (Gouel and Laborde 2019).

- *Vietnam's economy is growing quickly (7.02 percent in 2019) and transforming from an agrarian to a manufacturing and export-oriented economy at breathtaking pace* (IFAD 2019, 5). The time is opportune for aligning the "greening" of the economy while it is in take-off, based on lessons learned from industrial countries and best international practices. The timing is especially critical considering that Vietnam's phenomenal economic growth and development have been realized at the expense of the environment (IFAD 2019).

- *The relevance of "greening" the industrial policy and sector cannot be overstated: market access in export markets is tied increasingly to environmental requirements, particularly in high-income countries* (IFAD 2019)—most notably the European Union (EU) and the European Economic Area (EEA) (European Commission 2019). As an export-oriented economy with high trade openness, Vietnam is vulnerable to trade shocks, and yet the EU is a main trade partner (WTO 2020).

The impact of climate change on trade

Effects on productivity

Vietnam's agriculture sector accounts for 13.2 percent of exports and 10.3 percent of imports. It is especially vulnerable to climate change, notably rising temperatures and extreme weather events. In the absence of adaptation measures, yields will likely be reduced for rice, maize, cassava, sugarcane, coffee, and vegetables. Impacts are predicted to be more significant under dry scenarios than under wet ones. Hydrologic changes and sea-level rise will affect the availability of freshwater and may physically change the agricultural landscape. Climate change may also threaten the growth and reproduction of livestock and increase the incidence and spread of diseases (IFAD 2019, 44).

Effects on transportation

Transportation—specifically trade-related transport services—also could be adversely affected by extreme weather events. Sea-level rise may submerge some transportation infrastructure in coastal lowlands such as seaports, roads, railways, and airports. If the sea level rises 100 centimeters, about 4 percent of the national rail system, more than 9 percent of national highways, and about 12 percent of provincial roads will be affected; 28 percent of transportation systems in the Mekong Delta and 27 percent of provincial roads are at risk. Sea-level rise threatens the foundations of ports and airports in lowland coastal areas. Saltwater intrusion reduces the life expectancy of traffic works, especially steel structures, through the erosion of metal and other materials. High tides cause flooding, affecting the traffic and urban life of people, especially in the Mekong Delta (Nguyen et al. 2019, 59).

The impact of trade on climate change

Vietnam's export structure has shifted from predominantly primary goods to predominantly manufactured goods. Figure 6.1 shows the evolution of Vietnam's top five exports from 2007, when the country acceded to the World Trade Organization (WTO), to 2019. In 2007, Vietnam's export structure consisted mainly of primary goods—namely, petroleum and oils, coffee, and rice. By 2019, a dramatic shift had occurred in Vietnam's export structure, with its top exported products being radio telephony and transmission tools, automatic data-processing machines and parts, footwear, line telephony electrical apparatuses, and electronic integrated circuits and micro-assemblies. In contrast, Vietnam's import structure remains heavily dominated by petroleum products, which constituted nearly 60 percent of Vietnam's top five imports in 2019.

FIGURE 6.1 Evolution of Vietnam's Top Five Export Products, 2007–19

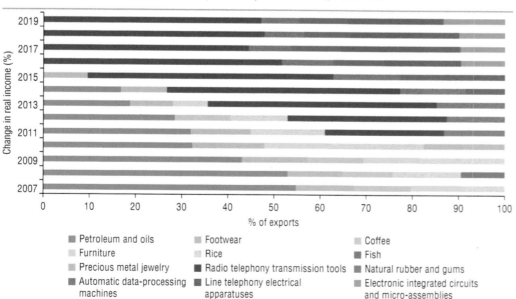

Source: COMTRADE (International Trade Statistics) database.
Note: Vietnam joined the World Trade Organization in 2007.

Vietnam's comparative advantages in goods (manufactured goods and agricultural products) and services (transport services) are in emissions- and energy-intensive sectors. The production of agricultural goods and transportation services has led to the degradation of natural capital and ecosystems, while also leading to a significant increase in mobility—the value of total passenger transportation per kilometer increased more than fivefold between 2000 and 2016, or by about 520 percent; during the same period, the total volume of national freight increased from 32 billion tons per kilometer to 111 billion tons per kilometer, or by about 340 percent. Such exponential growth in mobility has contributed to Vietnam's impressive economic growth and poverty reduction but also had negative environmental impacts (Oh et al. 2019).

The level of greenhouse gas emissions in Vietnam grew exponentially between 1990 and 2016. Total greenhouse gas emissions, including emissions from land use, have grown dramatically, from 50 million tons to more than 300 million tons. The combined emissions from oil extraction and agriculture have traditionally contributed more greenhouse gas emissions than industrial processes, which constituted nearly 50 percent of Vietnam's exports in 2019.

Vietnam's two most important economic sectors—industry and agriculture—are located in coastal lowlands and deltas, which are extremely vulnerable to the impact of climate change. Climate change will have a direct impact on the costs of production, while external trade policies will have an indirect impact on costs, as the country's main trade partners, particularly the EEA and the EU, begin to impose carbon border adjustments or carbon border taxes.

Recommendations

Effective domestic responses for decarbonization and adaptation measures are needed to ensure Vietnam's economic and trade resilience (UNCTAD 2021, 38). Vietnam can consider various trade measures for mitigating or adapting to the impact of climate change.

Explore options to diversify within sectors and into new sectors

The spectrum of diversification options can entail creating new by-products or expanding the portfolio of products shipped to Vietnam's major trading partners (UNCTAD 2021, 41). Closely connected to export diversification is transitioning from exports of primary products to higher value added products. Even if primary production in the agriculture and fisheries sectors experience climate-related declines, transitioning from exports of primary products to higher value added products downstream can maintain current levels of sectoral employment and revenue. The relevance of this option for an export-dependent country like Vietnam cannot be overstated.

Develop trade ties with nontraditional trade partners

Market diversification is closely connected to both export diversification and export value addition as the mechanism for adapting trade to climate change. A feasible prospect for a new trade partner or region whose environmental requirements for market access are not too stringent would be the African Continental Free Trade Area (AfCFTA)—the biggest free trade area in the world in terms of the number of participating countries.

Closely monitor developments in the environmental-climate requirements of Vietnam's main trade partners

Monitoring would allow Vietnam to anchor its trade policy or trade legal framework with that of its main trade partners (EU, EEA, and United States), which are increasingly interested in environmental sustainability. For example, by implementing a national carbon tax system, Vietnam's exports will be exempt from carbon border fees imposed by other countries (UNCTAD 2021, 38).

Gender mainstream climate change adaptation and mitigation-related trade laws and policies

Trade policy is not gender-neutral, considering that women and men play different roles in society and in the economy and enjoy different opportunities. Therefore, the distributional outcomes of trade are different for women than for men. If trade policies and measures are designed without considering their gender-specific outcomes, these policies risk magnifying existing gender gaps (UNCTAD 2017) and exacerbating the negative implications of climate shocks for women, particularly in rural areas. The Vietnamese government should prioritize gender mainstreaming in trade policies and laws in light of climate change. Such mainstreaming can be done by conducting ex ante gender impact assessments of trade measures and including gender considerations in the text of trade agreements, among others.

Participate more actively in the negotiation of international rules on environmental goods and services as well as their application

The WTO is currently the best forum for these negotiations. Vietnam is eligible for the benefits of special and differential treatment. This designation would help the country to (a) secure more time for transitioning to green standards set by high-income countries, while maintaining access to these markets; and (b) access funding and technical assistance from high-income countries as well as from the WTO (Aid for Trade) for the transition to green standards that are acceptable internationally. Furthermore, the WTO provides a viable forum for pursuing the elimination of trade measures and barriers, such as agricultural subsidies in high-income economies, which negatively affect Vietnam's trade performance. Finally, the WTO is a feasible avenue through which Vietnam could secure its global interests in environmental goods and services—for instance, by influencing the inclusion in the list of environmental goods and services categories in which Vietnam has a comparative advantage.

Ethiopia

Ethiopia is one of the most vulnerable countries to climate variability and climate change due to its heavy reliance on rain-fed agriculture and other primary commodities and natural resources and its limited capacity to deal with the potential adverse impacts. Ethiopia's challenges include the underdevelopment of water resources, weak health services, a high population growth rate, low economic development, inadequate road infrastructure in drought-prone areas, weak institutional structure, and lack of climate risk awareness (World Bank 2020b). Ethiopia has a complex geo-ecological setting, and virtually all of its ecosystems are fragile.

Key environmental and climate change issues especially relevant to the rural areas of Ethiopia include (a) climate variability and change, (b) land degradation and desertification, and (c) water scarcity and stress. The impacts of climate variability and climate change on rural populations and livelihoods, particularly in semiarid highlands and arid lowlands, are a priority concern. Extreme weather events are becoming more frequent, including intense droughts and floods in some areas, leading to lower crop yields or total crop failure, smaller livestock herds or more loss of livestock, diminished livelihoods of smallholder farmers and pastoralists, and heightened food insecurity.

The nexus of climate change and trade is particularly relevant for Ethiopia for the following reasons:

- *Climate change poses significant social, political, and economic risks to Ethiopia since the country is an agricultural economy, with the majority of its population employed in agriculture.* Notably, climate change will (a) alter comparative advantages and market dynamics in the agriculture sector to the detriment of low- and middle-income countries and major food-importing countries—of which Ethiopia is both (UNCTAD 2021, 12); (b) increase the costs of production and worsen the country's terms of trade and balance of payments; (c) increase unemployment; and (d) increase the risk of armed conflict and fragility.

- *Ethiopia is one of the fastest-growing economies in Africa and the world, with a nascent industrial sector experiencing rapid growth.*[1] In line with the theories on the climate-trade nexus, the time is opportune for aligning the "greening" of the economy while it is in take-off. Hence, Ethiopia is opportune for greening its nascent industrial policy based on lessons learned from industrial countries and best international practices. Greening the industrial sector is pertinent, as market access is tied increasingly to environmental requirements, particularly in high-income countries (mainly in the EEA and EU)—the biggest export markets for Ethiopia. There are plans to expand the scope of the EU CBAM policy to agricultural goods, and this could potentially affect Ethiopia's exports.

- *Ethiopia is a WTO observer state, in the process of acceding to the WTO.* The intricate relationship between the WTO and the trade-climate nexus gives more impetus for accelerating Ethiopia's WTO accession. Notably, the WTO is the premium forum in which global rules on climate change and trade are negotiated and implemented. Additionally, it is the most viable global forum for the enforcement of international environmental law.

- *Finally, an analysis of Ethiopia's challenges and opportunities could spur Ethiopia's interest in addressing climate change and trade.* Low- and middle-income countries have hardly participated in the negotiations of environmental goods and services, and conducting a cost-benefit analysis is critical, as is examining of the country's interests and how best to secure and promote them.

The impact of climate change on trade

Effects on productivity

The physical impacts of climate change will include adverse conditions for crop cultivation and livestock rearing. These impacts can have substantial effects not only on the production of primary agricultural and agroforestry commodities but also on the wider economy. In national economies with strong downstream linkages (like Ethiopia's), reductions in primary agricultural production can trickle down and affect productivity in downstream sectors, such as food processing and leather manufacturing, by reducing the availability and increasing the prices of primary inputs (UNCTAD 2021, 12).

The World Bank estimates that Ethiopia will lose more than 6 percent of each year's agricultural output if the current decline in average annual rainfall levels for primary agricultural zones continues to mid-century. Rising temperatures and shifting rainfall patterns may increase soil erosion, make it harder to grow many crops, and shorten the growing season. The livestock sector, a key economic sector for Ethiopia, is also likely to be affected by extreme weather conditions. Heat stress has many detrimental effects on livestock, but it can include reductions in milk production and reproduction, particularly for dairy cows. Extreme events, such as heat waves, may particularly affect beef and dairy cattle (UNCTAD 2021).

All regions around the world lose from reduced crop productivity (although a few individual countries may gain), but some are more than compensated by terms-of-trade gains. Because total food demand is inelastic, an average decrease in crop productivity will increase food prices substantially. Net-food-exporting regions (Latin America, Northern America, and Oceania) will benefit, and the burden of adjustment to climate change will fall to net-food-importing regions. Ethiopia is a significant food importer and is increasingly dependent on food aid, despite its comparative advantage in agricultural production (World Bank 2020b). Its balance of payments and the welfare of its people are also likely to be negatively affected.

Ethiopia is likely to lose its comparative advantage in the production of some agricultural products, although its comparative advantage in the production of others may be enhanced. Climate change will reshuffle global exporters and importers of agricultural products. Competitiveness effects are also likely to occur (UNCTAD 2021, 12).

Effects on communities

Remote and marginalized communities are likely to be the most affected by changes in future trade patterns due to climate change because they are dependent predominantly on pastoral and agropastoral livelihoods and are exposed to fragile and conflict-affected neighboring states—the so-called "emerging regions" of Ethiopia. The exposed regions include Amhara, Oromia, the Southern Nations, Nationalities and Peoples' Region, and Tigray. The emerging regions include Benishangul-Gumuz and Gambella in the western part of the country and the Afar and Somali regions in the east. While the emerging regions largely overlap with the arid lowlands, common features include (a) remoteness from the center and proximity to fragile neighboring states, (b) predominance of pastoral and agropastoral livelihoods, and (c) limited access to public services (including schools and clinics) and infrastructure (including roads), resulting in (d) low levels of literacy, formal education, and public health; (e) and widespread poverty (IFAD 2019, 2).

Effects on transport

Transport is likely to be affected substantially by extreme weather events. While this sector contributes heavily to greenhouse gas emissions, it also plays a crucial role in supporting Ethiopia's overall development strategy and supports its export and import networks. Given Ethiopia's topographical variations, which are characterized by extremely rugged terrain, the construction of transportation infrastructure tends to be physically difficult and costly. Continued repairs and maintenance are necessary to keep road networks functional. Maintaining such infrastructure could be difficult in conditions of higher rainfall, more flooding, and rising temperatures (World Bank 2020b).

Ethiopia is landlocked, and the port of Djibouti is the lifeline of Ethiopia's international trade. The volume of Ethiopian transit cargo that is handled by the port of Djibouti (85 percent of domestic cargo handled by the port) represents 95 percent of the volume of Ethiopian trade. The remaining 5 percent is handled by Port Sudan (World Bank 2018, 9). The port of Djibouti is experiencing the impacts of climate change. Sea-level rise is projected to lead to the loss of a sizable proportion of the northern and eastern coastlines due to a combination of inundation and erosion, with consequential risks for port infrastructure (World Bank 2021, 11).

Recommendations

Ethiopia could consider the following trade policy measures in mitigating and adapting to the impact of climate change.

Fast-track Ethiopia's accession to the WTO

WTO membership is essential for many reasons: it would enable Ethiopia to diversify its markets and exports, which is imperative for coping with climate shocks on trade (exports particularly), and would provide a forum for reaping the benefits of special and differential treatment to which Ethiopia is entitled as a low-income country. Differential treatment will be critical for securing more time for transitioning to green standards set by its main trade partners (the EU specifically) as well as for accessing resources (monetary and technical) for the transition.

The WTO provides a forum for eliminating trade measures and barriers, such as agricultural subsidies and tariff escalation, in the country's main export markets—factors that threaten Ethiopia's economic diversification of production.

WTO membership also would give Ethiopia a seat at the table where the global rules for environmental goods and services are being negotiated—giving Ethiopia a feasible avenue for securing its global interests in environmental goods and services. For instance, membership would give Ethiopia an opportunity to propose a list of environmental goods and services for which it has a comparative advantage, to be included in the WTO negotiating list.

WTO membership drives the liberalization of trade in environmental goods and services through tariffs and commitments encompassed in the accession process. Notably, WTO liberalization provides the government with an opportunity to tie domestic reforms for building a green economy with WTO accession. This is critical for countering domestic resistance to the green transition since the reforms are essentially an international obligation under international law.

Finally, WTO membership offers Ethiopia an avenue for becoming a signatory and state party to the Agreement on Trade-Related Aspects of Intellectual Property Rights (TRIPS). TRIPS is the most relevant international treaty governing intellectual property, and intellectual property is critical for transitioning to a green economy. The WTO (through its dispute settlement mechanism) offers a legal avenue for enforcing and fulfilling international environmental-climate treaties. WTO legal jurisprudence is critical for ensuring that progressive green jurisprudence becomes part of the domestic legal policy framework and would bolster efforts to reinforce the national legal framework for purposes of climate change adaptation and mitigation.

Enhance participation in subregional and regional trade organizations and agreements to which Ethiopia is a party

The multilateral trade system (underpinned by the WTO) has generally performed poorly in the liberalization of environmental goods and services, as evidenced by the stalled progress of the Environmental Goods Agreement negotiations. Regional economic organizations, specifically Asia-Pacific Economic Cooperation (APEC) and the EU, are making significantly more progress with regard to liberalization. The complications at the WTO are exacerbated by the current trade tensions among the most influential members of the organization. Additionally, regional economic organizations afford unique opportunities to diversify both goods and services (specifically, changes in comparative advantages in climate-related trade). In this regard, AfCFTA provides the greatest prospects for broadening or refocusing the spectrum of export markets as well as for redirecting exports to new markets where value added production is in greatest demand. Ethiopia's main trade partners are non-African states, and AfCFTA presents huge opportunities for improving market access, diversification, terms of trade, and industrialization as well as less stringent environmental and climate requirements than Ethiopia's main trade partners (the EU particularly).[2] For these reasons, enhanced subregional and regional trade offers significant opportunities. Even outside of AfCFTA, the manufacturing content of Africa's exports to Africa is much higher (46.3 percent) than that of its exports to the world (26.7 percent) (UNCTAD 2019, 20). In the same vein, even if primary production in the agriculture sector experiences climate-related declines, transitioning from exports of primary products to higher value added downstream products can maintain sectoral employment, revenue levels, and the overall value of sectoral exports, even as primary productivity declines (UNCTAD 2021, 41).

Closely monitor developments in the environment-climate requirements of its main trading partners

Monitoring would allow Ethiopia to anchor its own trade policy or trade legal framework strategically in accordance with that of its main trade partners (the EU and the United States), which are increasingly interested in environmental sustainability. For example, the exports of low- and middle-income countries that implement a national carbon tax system will be exempt from carbon border fees imposed by other countries (UNCTAD 2021, 38).

Notes

1. Six African countries are among the world's 10 fastest-growing economies: Rwanda (8.7 percent), Ethiopia (7.4 percent), Côte d'Ivoire (7.4 percent), Ghana (7.1 percent), Tanzania (6.8 percent), and Benin (6.7 percent) (AfDB 2020, 15).

2.   AfCFTA will have cascading effects. It will drive the structural transformation of economies—the transition from low-productivity, labor-intensive activities to higher-productivity, skills-intensive industrial and service activities—which, in turn, will produce better-paying jobs and reduce poverty. By promoting intra-African trade, the agreement will foster a more competitive manufacturing sector and promote economic diversification. The removal of tariffs will create a continental market that encourages companies to benefit from economies of scale and enable countries to accelerate their development (Signé 2020; World Bank 2020a, 21).

References

AfDB (African Development Bank Group). 2020. *African Economic Outlook 2020: Developing Africa's Workforce for the Future.* Abidjan: African Development Bank. https://www .africaeconomiczones.com/wp-content/uploads/2020/03/African-Economic-Outlook -2020-Developing-Africa%E2%80%99s-Workforce-for-the-Future.pdf.

European Commission. 2019. "The European Green Deal." Communication from the Commission to the European Parliament, the European Council, the European Economic and Social Committee, and the Committee of the Regions, European Commission, Brussels. https://ec.europa.eu/info/sites/info/files/european-green-deal-communication_en.pdf.

Gouel, Christophe, and David Laborde. 2019. "The Role of Trade in Adaptation to Climate Change." Vox EU, Centre for Economic Policy Research (CEPR), London. https://voxeu .org/article/role-trade-adaptation-climate-change.

IFAD (International Fund for Agricultural Development). 2019. "Socialist Republic of Viet Nam: Country Strategic Opportunities Programme (COSOP) 2019–2025." IFAD, Washington, DC.

Nguyen, Van Tue, Tang The Cuong, Nguyen Khac Hieu, Tran Thuc, Huynh Thi Lan Huong, Bui Huy Phung, Nguyen Mong Cuong, et al. 2019. "The Third National Communication of Vietnam to the UNFCCC." Government of Vietnam, Hanoi.

Oh, Jung Eun, Maria Cordeiro, John Allen Rogers, Khanh Nguyen, Daniel Bongardt, Ly Tuyet Dang, and Vu Anh Tuan. 2019. *Addressing Climate Change in Transport.* Vol. 1: *Pathway to Low-Carbon Transport.* Vietnam Transport Knowledge Series. Hanoi: World Bank. https:// openknowledge.worldbank.org/handle/10986/32411.

Signé, Landry. 2020. *Unlocking the Business Potential of Africa: Trends, Opportunities, Risks, and Strategies.* Washington, DC: Brookings Institution. https://www.brookings.edu/book /unlocking-africas-business-potential/.

UNCTAD (United Nations Conference on Trade and Development). 2017. *Making Trade Work for Gender Equality: From Evidence to Action.* Geneva: United Nations. https://unctad .org/meeting/making-trade-work-gender-equality-evidence-action.

UNCTAD (United Nations Conference on Trade and Development). 2019. *Key Statistics and Trends in Regional Trade in Africa.* Geneva: United Nations.

UNCTAD (United Nations Conference on Trade and Development). 2021. *Trade and Environment Review 2021: Trade Climate Readiness for Developing Countries.* Geneva: United Nations.

World Bank. 2018. "Port Development and Competition in East and Southern Africa: Prospects and Challenges, 2018." World Bank, Washington, DC. http://documents1.worldbank.org /curated/en/963231561663013431/pdf/Country-and-Port-Fact-Sheets-and-Projections .pdf.

World Bank. 2020a. *The African Continental Free Trade Area: Economic and Distributional Effects.* Washington, DC: World Bank. doi:10.1596/978-1-4648-1559-1.

World Bank. 2020b. "Climate Risk Country Profile: Ethiopia." World Bank Group, Washington, DC. https://climateknowledgeportal.worldbank.org/sites/default/files/2020-06/15463-WB _Ethiopia%20Country%20Profile-WEB_v2.pdf.

World Bank. 2021. "Climate Risk Country Profile: Djibouti." World Bank Group, Washington, DC. https://climateknowledgeportal.worldbank.org/sites/default/files/2021-02/15722-WB _Djibouti%20Country%20Profile-WEB.pdf.

World Bank and ADB (Asian Development Bank). 2020. "Climate Risk Country Profile: Vietnam." World Bank, Washington, DC; ADB, Metro Manila. https://climateknowledgeportal .worldbank.org/sites/default/files/2021-04/15077-Vietnam%20Country%20Profile-WEB .pdf.

WTO (World Trade Organization). 2020. "WTO Trade Profile: Viet Nam." WTO, Geneva. https://www.wto.org/english/res_e/statis_e/daily_update_e/trade_profiles/VN_e.pdf.

Appendix A

The 59 Countries with the Fastest-Growing Carbon Dioxide Emissions

TABLE A.1 Emerging Emitters, by Stage of Economic Development

Country	Low- and middle-income				Country	Low- and middle-income			
	Least developed	Landlocked	Developing	In transition		Least developed	Landlocked	Developing	In transition
Lao PDR	•	•	•		Kenya			•	
Myanmar	•		•		Uganda	•	•	•	
Zambia	•	•	•		Qatar			•	
Mozambique	•		•		Pakistan			•	
Tajikistan		•		•	Turkey			•	
Nepal	•	•	•		Indonesia			•	
Botswana		•	•		Mongolia		•		
Cambodia	•		•		Algeria			•	
Ethiopia	•	•	•		Jordan			•	
Sri Lanka			•		Iraq			•	
Georgia				•	Ghana			•	
Côte d'Ivoire			•		Eritrea	•		•	
Tanzania	•		•		Azerbaijan		•		•
Philippines			•		Namibia			•	
Congo, Dem. Rep.	•		•		Armenia		•	•	•
Mali	•	•	•		Colombia			•	
Haiti	•		•		Sudan	•		•	

Table continue next page

TABLE A.1 Emerging Emitters, by Stage of Economic Development *(Continued)*

Country	Low- and middle-income			
	Least developed	Landlocked	Developing	In transition
Bolivia		•	•	
Paraguay		•	•	
Nigeria			•	
Congo, Rep.			•	
Niger	•	•		
Bangladesh	•			
Kyrgyz Republic		•		•
Oman			•	
Guatemala			•	
Vietnam			•	
Senegal	•			
Benin	•			
Lebanon			•	
United Arab Emirates			•	
Saudi Arabia			•	
Chile			•	
Honduras			•	
Morocco			•	
Cameroon			•	
Angola	•			
Turkmenistan		•		•
Nicaragua			•	
Peru			•	
South Sudan	•	•		
Egypt, Arab Rep.			•	

Source: Adapted from Cui et al. 2020.

Reference

Cui, Can, Dabo Guan, Daoping Wang, Vicky Chemutai, and Paul Brenton. 2020. "Emerging Emitters and Global Carbon Mitigation Efforts." Working Paper, World Bank, Washington, DC. https://openknowledge.worldbank.org/handle/10986/35845.

Appendix B
Tariffs on Environmental Goods

FIGURE B.1 Average Most-Favored-Nation Tariffs on Environmental Goods (APEC List), by Economy, 2018

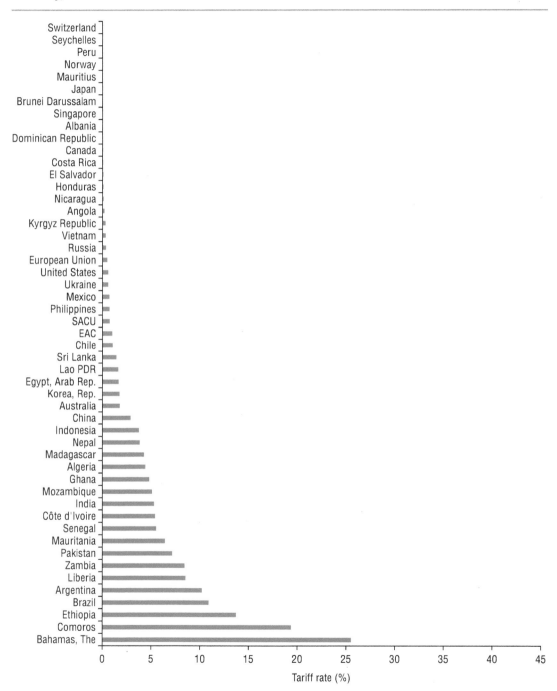

Source: Data from World Integrated World Integrated Trade Solution (WITS).
Note: APEC = Asia-Pacific Economic Cooperation; CEMAC = Central African Economic and Monetary Community; EAC = East African Community; GGC = Gulf Cooperation Council; SACU = Southern African Customs Union; WAEMU = West African Economic and Monetary Union.

FIGURE B.2 Average Most-Favored-Nation Tariffs on Environmentally Preferable Products, by Economy, 2018

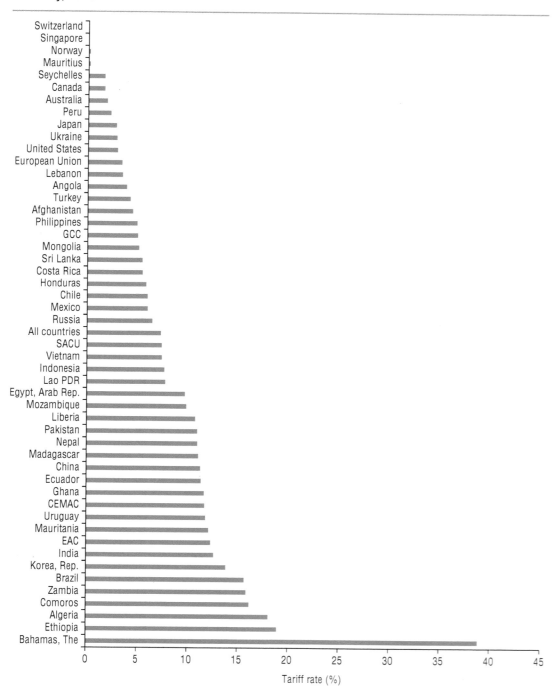

Source: Data from World Integrated World Integrated Trade Solution (WITS).

Note: APEC = Asia-Pacific Economic Cooperation; CEMAC = Central African Economic and Monetary Community; EAC = East African Community; GCC = Gulf Cooperation Council; SACU = Southern African Customs Union.

Appendix C
Climate and Trade Policy Diagnostic Framework

Introduction

(Brief description: This section should introduce the topic at hand—"climate change and trade"—and describe the objectives and the methodology of the country study.)

- What issues will be addressed in this country study?
- Why is "climate change and trade" relevant? Why is it relevant for this specific country?
- What is the objective of the country study? And which questions will be addressed throughout the paper?
- What research methodology will be used?

Country background

(Brief description: This section should provide succinct background information on the country, including its general economic profile, trade and climate frameworks, and any other background information relevant to the topic being addressed.)

1. **General economic profile**
   - Brief general description of the country, including its territory, geography, population, economic specialization, main economic indicators (gross domestic product [GDP], employment rate, and inflation rate)
   - Brief description of current economic situation of the country
   - Brief description of country's economic forecasts

2. **Country trade structure**
   - What is the current structure of trade, and how has it been evolving?
   - What are the key products that are imported and exported (goods and services)?
   - What are the main destinations for exports and sources for imports?

- What are the characteristics of the main transport routes for imports and exports?
- What are the main locations within the country where exports are produced (manufacturing, agriculture, services) and imports are used or consumed?

3. Country climate structure

- What have been the country's or region's trends in climate change?
- Trend in annual average temperature and precipitation for the country
- Variability in annual average temperature and precipitation across regions within the country
- Number and severity of extreme weather events
- Existing variations and corresponding livelihoods
- What is the country's share of global carbon dioxide (CO_2) emissions?
- Brief summary of the rules governing the country's climate structure. To what extent are these rules enforced?
- Did the country sign any international environmental treaties?

The impact of trade on climate change

(Brief description: This section should assess how the trade of goods and services within the country affects climate change and the climate impact of trade-related transportation services.)

1. Identify key tradable goods and services in which the country has a comparative advantage

- Are these goods and services from emissions- and energy-intensive sectors?
- Does the production of such goods and services lead to the degradation of natural capital and ecosystems—that is, deforestation, drought, others?
- Add a short box illustrating the adverse climate impact of trading certain goods, if there are good examples
- With evolving comparative advantages, what opportunities are available for the country to enter into the production and export of environmental goods, environmentally preferable products, and environmental services?
- What is the viability of the country's top trading sector (e.g., manufacturing) in the medium to long term with respect to the country's environmental objectives?

2. What are the main transport modes of the country's merchandise trade? By air, road, rail, sea?

3. What is the carbon footprint of transport services related to trading goods?

4. How are domestic policies adopted to boost trade affecting greenhouse gas emissions?

5. What are the potential impacts of domestic and overseas trade and climate change mitigation policies on trade, growth, and emissions? What are the distributional impacts?

6. What are the priority actions needed to build green competitiveness in the country's trading sectors?

The impact of a changing climate on trade

(Brief description: This section should identify key vulnerabilities in trade due to rising temperatures and other extreme weather events and analyze the ways in which current and future trade flows may be affected by climate change.)

1. Identify key goods and services that may be affected by rising temperatures and extreme weather events. Are these tradable goods and services? To which markets?

   • Review available studies on the impacts of climate change on tradable products for the country concerned

   • Add a short box illustrating adverse effects on a particular product, if there are good examples

   • Provide a time-series change (visualization) of production with 10–20-year intervals, if data are available

   • What products could be grown or made in this country, given the climate changes?

   • Which communities are likely to be affected by the changes in future trade patterns due to climate change?

2. What could be the potential impact of adverse climate conditions on trade-related infrastructures?

3. How are policies being adopted to reduce greenhouse gas emissions affecting production and trade?

   • Policies being adopted by the country or region itself

   • Policies being adopted in the main overseas markets

The role of trade in fostering climate mitigation and adaptation policies

(Brief description: This section should assess the role of trade, including access to new technologies, in fostering climate mitigation and adaptation policies.)

1. What opportunities exist for trade to contribute to adaptation and mitigation?

   • Climate-resilient infrastructure

   • Technological innovations (for example, drought-resistant seeds in agriculture, crop diversification, green technologies, and so on)

   • Sustainability standards, such as organic production and labeling

   • Laws and regulations

2. *What are the main policy and infrastructure barriers that limit the role of trade in mitigating and adapting to climate change?*

- Tariffs—on green goods and imported inputs crucial for diversification (seeds, for example)
- Nontariff barriers—for example, due to different standards and costly conformity assessment for imports embodying new technologies
- Poor trade facilitation
- Service trade restrictions

3. *How are transport and logistics infrastructure or services adapting to climate changes?*

- Is the transport infrastructure climate-resilient? How, and what percentage?
- Might ports become inundated?
- Is trucking congestion rampant? Have forests been cleared to expand the road network?
- What are the trade policies on importation of "green" transport goods and services? How restrictive?

4. *What are the distributional impacts of any trade policy and the climate impacts?*

- Which livelihoods?
- Which geographic area if activities are localized?
- Which communities (geographically) would have to adapt?
- Which communities might need to migrate because of adverse climate conditions?

5. *What are the potential implications for fragility and conflict in this area?*

- For instance, disaster risks from increased temperatures are expected to exacerbate existing tensions between communities for their household, agricultural, and livestock needs. Do those communities produce the same output?

Conclusions

(Brief description: This section should summarize the findings and recommend trade measures that can promote climate change mitigation and adaptation.)

1. *Summary of findings*

- How vulnerable is the country to extreme weather events?
- How did the country's trade policies affect its greenhouse gas emissions and climate change?
- How will the country's current and future trade flows be affected by climate change?

2. *Recommendations*

- Which trade measures can the country consider in mitigating or adapting to the impact of climate change?

- Can trade policy be used to mitigate the plight of the affected demographics from climate-change impacts—for example, minorities, women, and youth?

- Are concrete tools available to help the country ensure complementary of trade and climate policies?

- What are the priority technical assistance and capacity-building needs to support the efficient regulation of environmental goods and services?